Attracting BIRDS to your GARDEN

Attracting
BIRDS
to your
GARDEN

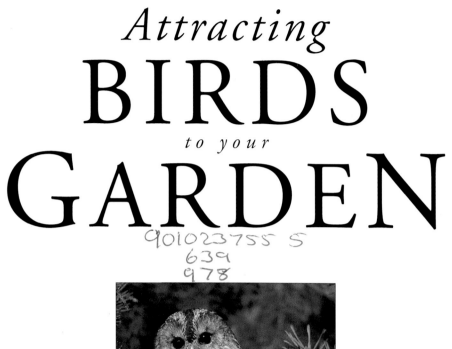

STEPHEN MOSS
and
DAVID COTTRIDGE

NEW
HOLLAND

This edition published in 2000 by
New Holland Publishers (UK) Ltd
London • Cape Town • Sydney • Auckland

24 Nutford Place
London W1H 6DQ
United Kingdom

80 McKenzie Street
Cape Town 8001
South Africa

14 Aquatic Drive
Frenchs Forest, NSW 2086
Australia

218 Lake Road
Northcote
Auckland
New Zealand

ISBN 1 85974 005 7

Commissioning Editor: Jo Hemmings
Design: Alan Marshall, Wilderness Design

Reproduction by Pica Colour Separation Overseas (Pte) Ltd
Printed and bound in Singapore by Tien Wah Press (Pte) Ltd

Jacket pictures

Front panel: (top left) Nuthatch
(middle left) Fieldfare
(bottom left) Bullfinch
(centre) Great Spotted Woodpecker
(top right) Great Tit and Blue Tit
(middle right) Blackbird
(bottom right) Feral Pigeon
Front panel vignettes: (left) Siskin
(right) Waxwing
Front flap: Jay
Spine: Robin
Back panel: Blue Tit
Back flap: Brambling

To my mother, Kay Moss, who loved her garden and its birds.

Author's Acknowledgements
Thanks go to the following people for their advice, help and informative comments and criticisms: Chris Harbard and Felicity Pryce-Page at the RSPB, Derek Toomer and Andrew Cannon at the BTO, and especially Chris Whittles at CJ Wildbird Foods.
Also thanks to Jo Hemmings and Sophie Bessemer at New Holland, for their hard work and relentless good humour in dealing with authors and photographers.
As always, to Jane for her love and support, and to Daniel, David and James, who put up with me working on the computer when they wanted to play Fantasy Football Manager, Doom and Chess.
Finally, I should like to thank my late mother, Kay Moss, my late grandmother, Edna Vale, and my aunt, Sally Rose, for encouraging my love of gardens – without forcing me to enjoy gardening.

Photographer's Acknowledgements
Special thanks to Alan Williams for supplying and acquiring photographs for the book.
Thanks are due to the following photographers: Richard Brooks, Hugh Clark, Dave Kjaer, C. Preston, Roger Tidman, Roger Wilmshurst
Nature Photographers: Derek Bonsall, Robin Bush, Michael Gore, R.T. Smith, Paul Sterry.
Windrush Photographic Agency: Arnoud van den Berg, Frank Blackburn, Dennis Green, John Hollis, B.R. Hughes, E.A. Janes, Chris Knights, Gordon Langsbury, J. Lawton-Roberts, Tim Loseby, Mark Lucas, D. Mason, George McCarthy, Alan Petty, Richard Revels, David Tipling, David Tomlinson, Maurice Walker.
Thanks also to the following who allowed use of their bird friendly gardens: Bob and Pat Bridges and Shirley and Maurice Carpenter in Chingford, John and Meg Whittles in Shropshire, Jo Hemmings in Greenwich.
Particular thanks to Chris Whittles of C.J. Wildbird Foods who supplied various bird feeders and bird food.
Special thanks to Oliver.

CONTENTS

CONTENTS

INTRODUCTION

WHY ATTRACT BIRDS TO YOUR GARDEN?

Birds have always been attracted to gardens, where they are able to find food, water and places to roost, nest and raise their young. You can help them by making your garden as attractive to birds as possible.

Britain is a nation of bird-lovers. The Royal Society for the Protection of Birds recently recruited its millionth member. Television programmes featuring our familiar native birds regularly top the ratings. Meanwhile, birdwatching is fast becoming one of our most popular pastimes. We are also a nation of gardeners. Every town has at least one garden centre, an industry with a national turnover of more than £3 billion a year. Newsagents' shelves are packed with gardening magazines, full of tips on how to improve your garden. And recently, when Geoff Hamilton, the best-known gardener on television, died suddenly, the nation mourned.

Put the two subjects together and you have this book. **Attracting Birds to Your Garden** is a practical guide, which will help you to do just that: attract a greater variety of birds to your garden by providing food, water, shelter and a place where they can nest and raise their young.

Gardens are a vital refuge for our birds. As natural habitats such as hedgerows, meadows and woodlands continue to disappear, our gardens are indispensable oases which help birds to survive and maintain their numbers. The food and water we provide is especially important during hard winter weather, or drought in summer.

But we don't just help garden birds for *their* sake. Watching birds in your garden provides endless hours of

Plants that can provide abundant food for hungry birds are essential, especially during the autumn and winter when natural food sources are often scarce. This Blackbird is tucking into a meal of rowan berries.

Woodland nesting birds such as this Great Tit have adapted very well to artificial nestboxes, where they can raise their young in a safe environment.

pleasure and delight, and helps you learn more about their day-to-day behaviour. As time goes by, you may find that your interest develops into a full-blown hobby, and you take up birdwatching farther afield.

How to Attract Birds to your Garden

So much for *why* we should attract birds to our garden – *how* do we do so? However large or small your garden, and whether it be in the centre of a city, a quiet suburb or the heart of the countryside, the same fundamental rules apply. Birds may vary from place to place and garden to garden, but their needs do not.

Among several things that attract birds to a garden, four stand out as most important:

- **food:** to provide the energy needed to survive, especially during harsh winter weather.
- **water:** for drinking and bathing.
- **shelter:** places in which to roost at night; and somewhere to build a nest and raise young during the breeding season.
- **safety:** an environment in which they can carry out these activities without danger from poisoning, pests or predators.

As a garden-owner, you have a responsibility to the birds to provide these four basic requirements. Doing so will

A typical suburban garden, with a number of features designed to attract birds, including mature trees, shrubs to provide cover for nesting and roosting, and a pond.

Birds obtain much of their energy from natural food sources, such as insects which feed on native plants. This Whitethroat is tucking into a juicy spider.

take a little time, money and effort – but will certainly be worth it in the end.

There are several stages in the process of creating a 'bird-friendly' garden:

1. **Planning:** you need to decide *what* you are going to do, *how,* and by *when.*
2. **Planting:** to create areas where birds can roost and nest, and plants which produce fruit or berries, or attract insects for the birds to eat.
3. **Feeding:** to provide a range of food to attract a wide variety of different species with different feeding requirements, throughout the year.
4. **Providing nest sites:** such as nestboxes, for birds to use as a substitute when natural sites are not available or are in short supply.

Food provided by people is often a lifesaver for wild birds. This Great Spotted Woodpecker is taking peanuts from a sturdy metal feeder sited where cats cannot reach it.

How to Use this Book

Attracting Birds to Your Garden is divided into two main parts:

Part 1 (Chapters 1–5) contains advice and information on how to make your garden more attractive to birds. It contains step-by-step illustrations that will enable you to adapt your garden to the needs of wildlife, and it covers planning and planting, feeding, water in the garden, nesting, and pests, predators and other hazards of the garden environment.

Part 2 (Chapter 6) is a comprehensive **Directory of Garden Birds**, with text and illustrations of eighty different species. This will enable you to identify the birds that visit your garden and to find out more about how they live – their dietary and environmental needs, how they nest and how they raise their young.

SUMMARY OF CHAPTERS

Chapter 1, Planning the Garden is a step-by-step guide to creating a 'bird-friendly' garden. It gives advice on the birds' seasons, garden design for birds, the best plants to grow, and how to create a wild garden. There is also advice on observing and recording the birds that visit your garden, and how you can join a national survey of garden birds.

In early autumn, elderberries provide a convenient and accessible food resource for all kinds of birds.

Chapter 2, Feeding Garden Birds covers the two main ways in which you can provide food: by stocking your garden with plants that provide fruits and berries and attract insects; and by putting out food such as nuts and seeds to supplement the natural food supply. It gives details of the many different artificial feeders, and new range of foods on the market, and examines whether or not you should continue feeding birds during the spring and summer.

Chapter 3, Water in the Garden explains why we need to provide water for the birds: for drinking and bathing. There is advice on how to make or buy a bird bath; and how to plan, make, plant, stock and maintain a garden pond. The dangers of garden ponds, and how to safeguard children against drowning, are also covered.

Chapter 4, Nesting includes an explanation of the breeding cycle of birds, including birdsong and territory, nest-building, egg-laying and incubation, hatching and feeding young, and fledging chicks. There are details of which plants are most suitable for nesting birds, together with how to make, buy, site, and maintain a nestbox. There is also information on how you can participate in a national survey of nesting birds – the British Trust for Ornithology's Garden BirdWatch.

Chapter 5, Pests and Predators looks at some of the threats facing garden birds, including domestic cats, squirrels, and bird predators such as the Sparrowhawk, Jay and Magpie. There are tips on dealing with insect pests and the use of pesticides. There is also advice on how to deal with young birds that fall from the nest, and how to get advice from the RSPB's Enquiry Unit.

BIRD TOPOGRAPHY

Bird topography is, at its most basic level, the way in which we are able to describe precisely the external features of a bird. Although topography mainly applies to the various different parts of a bird's plumage, it also includes those areas known as the 'bare parts' – the bird's beak, legs and feet.

At first sight, learning bird topography might appear to be a difficult, even pointless, exercise, full of complicated terms such as 'lores', 'supercilium' and 'greater coverts'. You may wonder why such precise descriptions are necessary, when after all, most birdwatchers are able to describe a bird's appearance using general terms such as 'upperparts' and 'underparts'.

However, delve a little deeper into the subject, and you'll soon discover that a good working knowledge of bird topography can help you gain a greater understanding into many fascinating areas, including identification, behaviour and evolution.

The main way in which birdwatchers use bird topography is to help them identify a particular species of bird. Detailed knowledge of a bird's plumage is invaluable when it comes to distinguishing individuals from similar and closely related species, such as warblers, or birds of prey.

Bird topography can also help you decide the age and sex of a bird. For example, as gulls mature, they moult – gradually exchanging one set of feathers for another. By examining the different feather patterns, experienced birdwatchers can tell if a bird is a juvenile, or a 'first-winter' individual, 'second-summer', and so on.

Finally, an understanding of bird topography will help you appreciate that although some groups of feathers may be more noticeable than others, the basic patterns of bird's plumages are the same. This is because whatever the species, large or small, brightly coloured or drab, all birds share the same evolutionary history. So next time you watch a finch or a tit on your garden feeder, take a closer look.

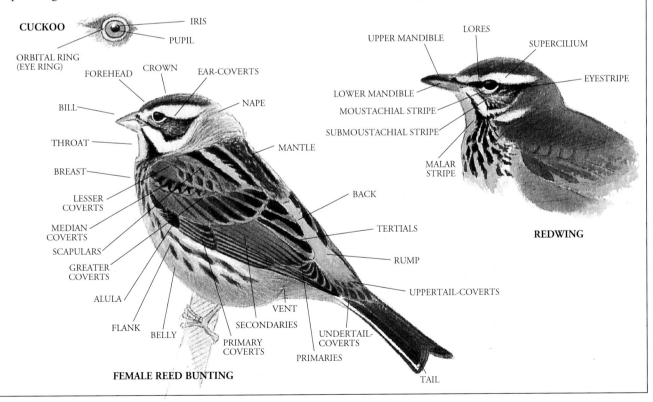

CUCKOO
IRIS
PUPIL
ORBITAL RING (EYE RING)
FOREHEAD
CROWN
EAR-COVERTS
BILL
NAPE
THROAT
MANTLE
BREAST
LESSER COVERTS
MEDIAN COVERTS
SCAPULARS
GREATER COVERTS
ALULA
BACK
TERTIALS
RUMP
UPPERTAIL-COVERTS
FLANK
BELLY
VENT
SECONDARIES
PRIMARY COVERTS
PRIMARIES
UNDERTAIL-COVERTS
TAIL
FEMALE REED BUNTING

UPPER MANDIBLE
LORES
SUPERCILIUM
EYESTRIPE
LOWER MANDIBLE
MOUSTACHIAL STRIPE
SUBMOUSTACHIAL STRIPE
MALAR STRIPE
REDWING

1

PLANNING THE GARDEN

In the garden the difference between pleasure and pain is, to a great extent, knowledge.

JANE FEARNLEY-WHITTINGSTALL,
GARDENING MADE EASY

WHY BIRDS NEED GARDENS

Until the coming of humans, Britain was a land of woods and forests, with trees covering most of the lowland landscape. We know very little about the birdlife of that prehistoric era, but it is likely that forest species such as tits and woodpeckers thrived, while birds of open country, like larks and pipits, were much less common and widespread than today.

PREHISTORIC BRITAIN AND ITS BIRDS

The arrival of people changed the face of the landscape forever. By cutting down trees for fuel and clearing forests to plant crops, the early settlers created a more open landscape. However, human influence was not entirely destructive, as the coppicing of woodlands and making of hay meadows created new habitats for birds.

For several thousand years, people and birds lived alongside each other more or less in a state of harmony, notwithstanding the hunting activities of prehistoric people. Then, two centuries ago, everything changed, with the coming of the Industrial Revolution. Britain's population increased rapidly, and new towns and cities were built to support the extra people and the new industries in which they worked. For the first time since the arrival of humans on these islands, the future of Britain's birdlife was under threat.

TWENTIETH-CENTURY DESTRUCTION

The twentieth century has seen a huge acceleration in the rate of habitat destruction by farming and the building of roads, towns and cities. It is estimated that since World War II Britain has lost 95% of its hay and wildflower meadows, 80% of its chalk and limestone downs, and more than half of its ancient woodland. Once destroyed, these complex habitats can never be fully recovered.

One of the very few compensations has been the rise of the private garden. Gardens in the United Kingdom

Today, much of the countryside is given over to large-scale arable farming, which supports few birds. So our gardens provide an essential refuge to help the birds survive.

now occupy a land area equivalent to over 400,000 hectares (1 million acres or more than 1,500 square miles) – an area larger than the county of Suffolk.

As a result, our gardens have become a substitute habitat for many birds whose original habitat is under threat. Blue and Great Tits, Robin, Blackbird and Song Thrush are all originally woodland species that now depend a great deal on gardens for food, roosting and nesting sites.

As modern agricultural practices continue to turn much of our countryside into a sterile wasteland virtually devoid of birds, gardens are more important than ever. This is especially true for seed-eating species such as sparrows, finches and buntings.

Meanwhile, in the last decade or so, a new threat has arisen: global warming. As the world's climate begins to warm up, and habitats change more rapidly than ever before, our gardens are likely to be among the few oases of relative stability in a rapidly changing landscape.

Traditional hay-meadows such as this one in the English Midlands are becoming a rare sight. You can help redress the balance by letting part of your garden go wild.

FALLS AND RISES

All our breeding and wintering birds, however common and familiar, are now under threat. Even the House Sparrow, for so long taken for granted, is showing signs of population decline, especially in rural areas.

The Song Thrush population has fallen by more than half in just thirty years, and the species has joined once-familiar garden visitors, such as the Turtle Dove, Spotted Flycatcher and Bullfinch, on the RSPB's latest 'Red list', which features birds of particularly high conservation concern.

Fortunately, it is not all bad news. In the last few years, the Sparrowhawk has made an astonishing comeback following its dramatic decline after the end of World War II, which was caused by the widespread use of lethal agricultural pesticides such as DDT. Today, this dashing predator is becoming a familiar sight in many gardens.

Siskins, birds which were once rare visitors to the garden, are now found in more than two-thirds of gardens surveyed. They are usually attracted by

On the way down: the Song Thrush, once a common and familiar species, has recently suffered a rapid and serious decline in numbers. This is almost certainly due to modern farming methods, which reduce the supply of available food.

On the way up: the Collared Dove, unknown in western Europe before World War II, is now one of the most common garden birds. Its monotonous cooing call can be heard throughout rural and suburban areas.

the widespread provision by householders of their favourite food, peanuts. And another newcomer, the Collared Dove, has recently entered the list of Britain's 'top ten' garden birds.

THE BIRDS' SEASONS

When planning your garden with the intention of attracting birds, it is essential to understand how the different seasons of the year influence their lives.

The behaviour of birds is strongly governed by the seasonal cycle, especially the changes in daylight. The lengthening spring days are the trigger for birds to begin breeding; whereas in the autumn, decreasing day-length is the signal for migrants like Swifts and Swallows to head south for the winter.

Hard winter weather is a very important influence on bird populations, especially for smaller species, such as the Wren. Drought or heavy rainfall during the breeding season also affect breeding success. In fact, there is

In winter, small birds like this Blue Tit need to eat about one quarter of their body weight every day in order to survive. So they depend largely on food provided by humans.

Summer visitors such as this Spotted Flycatcher may not arrive back to Europe from their African wintering-quarters until late April or even May.

almost no aspect of birds' lives that is not governed by the calendar. But that is not to say that the seasonal cycles of birds follow our own. Breeding behaviour can begin as early as January, while some species, such as the Woodpigeon, seem to have no season – they have been recorded laying eggs in almost every month of the year.

Some migrants, such as the Chiffchaff and Blackcap, return as early as March, while others, including the Swift and Spotted Flycatcher, do not reach our shores until late April or May.

Moreover, the timing of these events varies not only from species to species but also from place to place. For example, Swallows in the south of England usually return to their nesting sites by the middle of April, whereas those nesting in the north of Scotland may not arrive until two or even three weeks later.

Finally, the breeding season may also vary from year to year, depending on the weather. A spell of unseasonably warm weather in March will hasten its start, but if the weather is particularly cold or wet, nesting activity may be delayed by a month or more. This is especially true of birds that feed on flying insects, such as the Swift, which, during the late spring of 1996 did not begin egg-laying until June.

Although things are far from clear cut, it is possible to identify three main – if overlapping – seasons, shown in the table on the left.

HOW TO PLAN YOUR GARDEN FOR BIRDS

This section assumes that you already have a garden, and that you are not starting completely from scratch. If you

THE BIRDS' CALENDAR

SEASON	TIME OF YEAR	MAIN ACTIVITIES
Winter	November–March	Feeding Survival
Breeding	February–July	Courtship Nest-building Egg-laying Raising young
Post-breeding	July–November	Moulting Preparation for winter Migration & local movements

have a totally blank canvas to work on, there are a number of excellent garden planning books to help you (*see* list on page 156).

ALL CHANGE?

There are some things you cannot change about your garden: its location (urban, suburban or rural), its size and shape, and the immediate surroundings.

Other things are difficult to change. If you don't have any mature trees, you'll have to wait a very long time after planting them before you see the results of your labours. So be realistic about your ambitions.

Despite these constraints, there are all kinds of things you *can* do. With a little time and effort these will yield the results you're hoping for, and attract a wider variety of birds to your garden.

This chapter will take you through some of the basics involved in planning and planting a garden to attract birds. Providing food, water and nest sites are all covered in later chapters.

TAKING STOCK

At the beginning, it is well worth taking time to assess what your garden already has, what is missing, and how you might make improvements. Draw a rough plan of your garden, and mark which of the following features it already contains:

- terrace or patio areas
- lawn
- flower beds
- shrubs and bushes
- mature trees
- pond
- wilderness area

The ideal bird garden should contain all of these, though many gardens will have only the first three or four features on the list.

The next step is to think about how you are going to change the emphasis in your garden, favouring features which will attract more birds – those towards the bottom of the list. The change doesn't need to be drastic – after all, you'll want to keep features like flower beds and a lawn for your own pleasure, as well as for the birds.

One way to change the emphasis is to alter the proportions of land area given over to each feature. So, for example, can you bear to lose part of your lawn to create a pond or wilderness area? Can some of the flower beds be replanted with shrubs for nesting birds? Can some of the terrace be given over to climbing plants such as clematis or honeysuckle, suitable for roosting or nesting?

MAKING PLANS

First take the rough plan of your garden and draw it up neatly, trying to keep measurements and positions as accurate as possible. Then take a similar-sized piece of paper, and trace onto it the features which won't change position: e.g. the terrace, mature trees.

The next step is to experiment with different ideas for your new garden design. Don't be afraid to consider radical changes as well as simple ones, but make sure you discuss the ideas with other members of your household before you start digging!

To get an idea, take a look at the 'before and after' designs shown here. Even though your own garden may be different in size and shape, the same basic principles will hold true.

Even a small suburban garden can be planned to attract a wide variety of birds. This garden has a good range of shrubs and bushes for birds to feed, roost and build their nests.

THE BIRD-UNFRIENDLY GARDEN

Lack of imagination and effort will result in a sterile, hostile environment, attracting few birds. Straight lines dominate, creating isolated, unproductive areas. Note the lack of suitable food plants, bird tables, bird feeders, or places to nest and roost.

Key:

A. Large, well-manicured lawn.

B Long, narrow flower-beds, planted with exotic, non-native flowering plants unsuitable for birds.

C Thick, coniferous hedge, suitable for roosting but little else.

D Bare garden fence, without any climbing plants.

E Terrace.

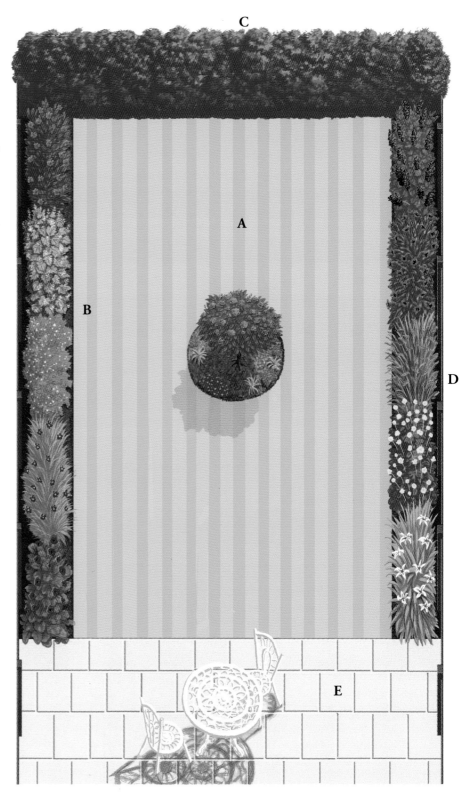

THE BIRD-FRIENDLY GARDEN

With a little thought, planning and effort, any garden can be transformed into a welcoming, friendly environment to attract birds. Note the absence of straight lines, and the gradual shift from one area to another, creating a continuous series of mini-habitats.

Key:

A Much smaller lawn area, with suitably-placed bird table and bird bath.

B Wider, more varied flower-beds, with a range of native flowers for feeding, and climbing plants to use as nest-sites.

C Large area of native shrubs and bushes, for nesting, roosting and feeding.

D Wilderness area at the back, with small hay-meadow and seed-bearing plants.

E Small pond, with marshy edges, creating mini-wetland habitat.

F Rockery, with plenty of gaps to conceal invertebrates.

G Bird table, bird bath, feeding stations and nestboxes, to provide for the widest possible variety of species throughout the year.

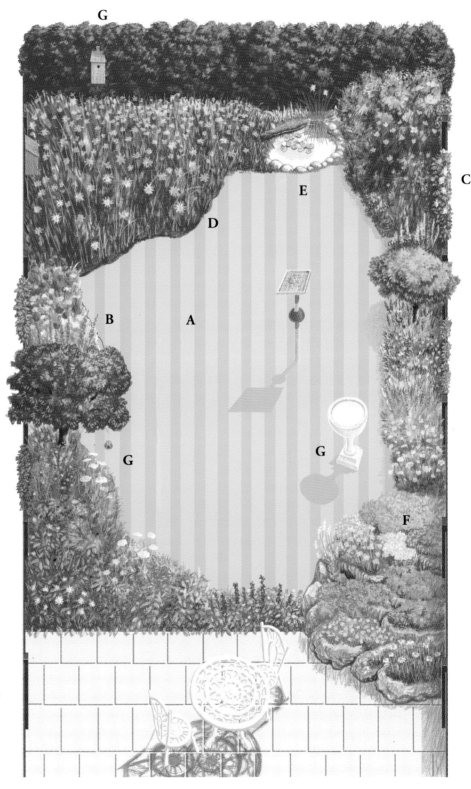

PLANTS TO ATTRACT BIRDS

You should plant trees, hedges, bushes, shrubs and flowering plants in your garden for four main reasons:

- to provide food for the birds directly, in the form of seeds, fruits and berries;
- to provide food indirectly, in the form of insects and other invertebrates which are attracted to these plants;
- to provide shelter, either at night for roosting, or during bad weather;
- to provide natural nesting sites.

In each case, by providing a greater variety of plants, you will be providing a greater variety of different foods and types of nest sites, and so attract the widest possible range of different species of birds.

TREES AND HEDGES

Large, mature trees and well-established hedges are among the most valuable of all bird habitats, because of the diversity of food, and the many opportunities for roosting and nesting, that they provide.

A single oak tree may support more than two hundred different species of invertebrates, which in turn attract a wide variety of different birds. Oaks also produce acorns, a favourite food of, among others, Jays.

Other native trees such as birch, beech, alder and willow attract all sorts of creepy-crawlies, and also produce food in the form of catkins, nuts and cones, especially favoured by finches such as Siskins and Redpolls. Fruit trees such as apple, pear and crab apple

Mature trees provide essential nest-sites for scarce, hole-nesting birds such as this Lesser Spotted Woodpecker.

are also popular, take up less space, and have a fairly rapid growth rate.

If your garden is not large enough to support trees, why not plant a hedge? In our countryside, many thousands of miles of hedgerow have been destroyed since the end of World War II in the cause of greater agricultural efficiency. This has meant the loss of a huge amount of nesting cover for birds. By planting even a small hedge of hawthorn, privet or laurel, you will provide excellent cover for nesting birds such as the Robin, the Dunnock or the Wren.

It is best to avoid most popular non-native trees, such as the sycamore, horse chestnut, sweet chestnut and various types of flowering cherry. Although these grow quickly and look very attractive, their foreign origin means that they support very few species of native insects and other invertebrates.

A few non-native plants, such as the evergreen Leyland cypress, are suitable for birds like Greenfinches, which roost and nest in their dense foliage. However, remember that these grow very quickly, and if you're not careful may soon take over your garden!

BUSHES AND SHRUBS

Bushes and shrubs are among the most valuable habitat for garden birds, as they provide two of the most important factors in a bird-friendly garden: food and shelter. Most bushes and shrubs are fairly fast-growing, and can be purchased from your local garden centre or grown from cuttings.

The ideal bushes and shrubs are those native, flowering varieties such as

Pussy willow catkins come out early in the year, providing valuable food for wintering birds.

Mature trees like this oak support a huge variety of insects and other invertebrates, which in turn provide lots of food for hungry birds.

elder and hawthorn, which produce plenty of succulent fruits and berries for birds to eat through the autumn and winter *(see below).*

If your garden is tight for space, consider planting climbers such as ivy, clematis and honeysuckle, or bushes such as forsythia or yew. All these will provide a variety of food and cover, vital for birds throughout the year.

FLOWERING PLANTS

All kinds of flowering plants are attractive to birds: either because of the nectar in the flowers themselves, or because they produce an abundance of seeds at the end of the flowering season. Good seed-bearing flowers include foxglove, honesty, and sunflower, which grows well in any sheltered, sunny part of the garden.

Native wild flowers, such as the primrose and the red campion are also popular with some birds because they attract the caterpillars of butterflies and moths. These are the staple diet of Blue and Great Tit chicks. Another plant that will attract butterflies is the attractive buddleia, often called the butterfly bush, whose purple flowers appear around midsummer.

Many plants come under the notorious category of weeds, although, as my mother always used to say, "a weed is just a flower in the wrong place". In fact, the bird garden is the right place for many so-called weeds, as native plants such as stinging nettle, dandelion and teasel

The perfect bird garden? The owner has provided plenty of trees and shrubs, as well as a well-stocked bird table and bird bath.

produce valuable seeds for birds to eat, and are an an essential part of any 'wildlife garden' *(see below).*

In addition, many popular non-native garden plants such as cornflower, honesty and forget-me-not also produce suitable seeds – and they look attractive.

LAWNS, ROCKERIES AND TERRACES

A lawn has a valuable place in a bird garden, as it will attract a wide variety of ground-feeding birds. Blackbirds,

The seeds from alder cones are a favourite food of the Siskin. They are also attracted to seeds from spruce, pine and birch.

So-called 'weeds' like this thistle are ideal for finches like this Linnet, as they provide plenty of energy-giving seeds.

The lawn is a valuable part of any bird-friendly garden, as it attracts birds like this Green Woodpecker, which probes into the short grass in search of ants.

Robins and Song Thrushes come to feed on worms, while other species, such as Starlings, Dunnocks and Pied Wagtails, will search for small insects and other invertebrates. If you're really lucky, a Green Woodpecker may drop in to look for its staple diet of ants.

During hot, dry weather in summer, keep your lawn well watered, as this will bring organisms such as earthworms to the surface. During the winter, a lawn is a good place to put fruit such as rotting apples, which is ideal for Blackbirds and winter thrushes.

Paved areas such as a rockery or a patio or terrace are less important, although birds will still use them. The gaps between rocks and paving-stones often support insects such as ants, and Song Thrushes need a hard area to use as an 'anvil' on which to smash snails, their

Berries are an essential food source for many birds, especially during the winter when other food is scarce. This Waxwing is tucking into hawthorn berries.

Birds like blackberries, too! This Greenfinch will get valuable energy, enabling it to survive the winter cold.

favourite prey. Finally, a south-facing rockery is an ideal place for birds to sun themselves after bathing.

FRUITS AND BERRIES

The fruits of flowering plants, or berries as they are often called, are a high-energy food, favoured by many different kinds of birds. Berries are especially popular during spells of harsh winter weather, when other sources of food become scarce. Berries often attract winter thrushes such as the Fieldfare and Redwing, or if you're really lucky, a wandering flock of Waxwings!

Birds and berries are a remarkable example of interaction in nature. The fleshy pulp of a berry conceals and protects the seeds within. But it has another, more crucial role. Berries attract hungry birds, which provide the means for the precious seeds contained inside to be spread over a wider area. As birds move from one place to another, they drop or excrete some of the undigested seeds, thus helping the parent plant to spread and multiply. The plant benefits by having its seeds distributed, while the bird gets a nourishing meal!

From the gardener's point of view, fruits and berries make plants look attractive during autumn and winter when the rest of the garden may not be looking its best.

TYPES OF BERRY

In the British Isles, more than sixty native species of plants bear fleshy fruits:
- **trees**, such as yew, holly, hawthorn, blackthorn, crab-apple and elderberry.
- **shrubs**, such as juniper, blackberry (bramble), dog rose and privet.

Native plants like this blackthorn are ideal for birds such as warblers, finches and thrushes to build their nests.

All sorts of fruit-bearing plants are valuable to birds, such as this pretty autumn-fruiting rosehip.

- **climbing plants**, such as ivy and honeysuckle.
- **herbaceous plants**, such as lily-of-the-valley and lords and ladies (the arum lily).
- one **parasitic epiphyte**, the mistletoe.

Many of these plants will grow readily in gardens. In addition, there are a number of introduced, non-native species which produce fruits that are attractive to birds. These include the various species of berberis and cotoneaster, firethorn (pyracantha), and non-native varieties of honeysuckle and yew.

TIMING OF BERRY PRODUCTION

A great advantage of berries is their seasonality. Different plants fruit at different times of year, so if you plant a good range of fruiting species you can ensure that there will always be a ready-made food supply available for the birds. The peak season for berry production runs from August to January. Planting shrubs and trees that fruit throughout this season will thus ensure natural food at a critical time for the birds' survival.

Some plants, like the wild cherry, have a very brief fruiting season, running for just a couple of months in midsummer. Others, like the blackberry and elder, fruit in autumn, the time when there is most natural food available for the birds.

Perhaps the best berry-bearing plants are those with a long fruiting season extending into late winter, when food is in the shortest supply. These are mainly evergreen plants such as mistletoe, ivy and holly, whose fruiting season may begin in September and continue until the following July. The hawthorn also has a long fruiting season, from August until March or April.

BIRDS THAT FEED ON BERRIES

A dozen or so birds regularly feed on berries in gardens. The champion fruit-eaters are our three native and two wintering thrushes: Blackbird, Song Thrush, Mistle Thrush (named after its preference for mistletoe), Redwing and Fieldfare. Without the widespread availability of berries, both inside and outside gardens, these birds would find it hard to obtain the energy needed to survive long spells of freezing weather in winter.

The larger species of warbler, such as Whitethroat, Lesser Whitethroat, Garden Warbler and Blackcap, are very partial to fruit, especially during the autumn, when they need to build up their resources of energy before undertaking the long journey south. The recent increase in wintering by central European Blackcaps in the British

Hawthorn berries are attractive to birds as well as humans. The hawthorn provides berries from late summer until the following April, making it a very valuable food plant for birds such as thrushes.

The Great Tit is the largest and one of the most familiar members of the tit family, and is particularly partial to the dark purple elderberry.

Isles, has undoubtedly been helped by the ability of the species to feed on berries.

Other species, such as Robin, Starling, Woodpigeon and various species of finch also regularly feed on berries.

Perhaps the most attractive and spectacular fruit-eater is the rare Waxwing, an occasional winter visitor to the British Isles. Waxwings breed in the far north of Scandinavia and Russia, where they raise their young on the abundance of flying insects there. However, in winter they subsist almost entirely on berries.

During some years, the berry crop fails, forcing large flocks of Waxwings to head south and west towards the British Isles in search of food. These 'irruptions', as they are called, sometimes involve thousands of birds, some of which may suddenly turn up in gardens to feed on berries. A single bird, feeding on a cotoneaster, was estimated to have eaten between 600–1000 berries in a single day – more than twice its body weight!

If you are interested in learning more about this fascinating subject, it is well worth getting hold of the excellent book 'Birds and Berries', by Barbara and David Snow (*see* page 156).

Natural Food: Insects and other Invertebrates

One very good reason to grow a wide variety of native garden plants is that they attract insects and other invertebrates, including butterfly and moth caterpillars, spiders, slugs and snails, beetles, grubs and other larvae.

Insects are the staple diet of many birds, including warblers, Robin, Dunnock and the aptly named flycatchers. Other species such as tits, which normally eat seeds and nuts, prefer to feed their young on live food such as caterpillars. So an abundance of insect food is especially important during spring and summer, when the birds are breeding.

To attract a good variety of invertebrate food, it is best to grow native plants. Alien species such as the sycamore may look attractive, but they harbour far fewer species of insects than their native cousins such as the oak or ash.

Shrubs and bushes such as bramble, honeysuckle and elder provide plenty of blossom in spring, attracting all sorts of insects – and the birds that prey on them.

Many butterflies and moths choose particular species of plant on which to lay their eggs, so that their caterpillars have an ample supply of food when they hatch. Wildlife gardener Chris Baines recommends the following food plants to attract breeding butterflies:

- **stinging nettles**: small tortoiseshell, red admiral, comma, peacock and painted lady.
- **nasturtium**: large white.
- **buckthorn**: brimstone.
- **hop**: comma.
- **hedge mustard**: large white, small white, orange-tip.

Many gardeners take a very different view of insects, slugs and snails, as these creatures feed on garden plants, causing damage and occasionally outright destruction. However, you can strike a balance between preserving your precious plants and encouraging natural food for the birds (*see* Chapter 5 for further details).

Flowering plants attract a wide range of insects, including butterflies such as this Small Tortoiseshell, feeding on a Michaelmas Daisy.

TABLE OF SUGGESTED PLANTS AND THEIR USES

NATIVE PLANTS:				
ENGLISH NAME(S)	SCIENTIFIC NAME(S)	TYPE OF PLANT	KEY FEATURES	TO ATTRACT
Alder	*Alnus glutinosa*	Tree	Catkins Cones (autumn/winter)	Finches, especially Siskin, Redpoll and Goldfinch; tits
Apple	*Malus* (various varieties)	Tree	Blossom (spring) Fruit (autumn)	Thrushes, especially Blackbird (feeding); Goldfinch (nesting)
Beech	*Fagus sylvatica*	Tree	Beech-mast (autumn)	Finches, especially Chaffinch & Brambling; Nuthatch, tits, woodpeckers
Bramble, Blackberry	*Rubus fruticosus*	Bush	Fruit (autumn) Cover for nesting	Blackbird, thrushes, warblers
Crab apple	*Malus sylvestris* (and various non-native species)	Bush or small tree	Insects (spring/summer) Fruit (autumn)	Various species, including thrushes and Ring-necked Parakeet
Elder	*Sambucus nigra*	Bush	Flowers (summer) Berries (autumn) Cover for nesting	Thrushes, Woodpigeon (feeding) Various species, including warblers (nesting)
Hawthorn	*Crataegus monogyna*	Bush or hedge	Insects (spring/summer) Berries (autumn) Cover for nesting	Various species, including thrushes, Woodpigeon (feeding) Various species (nesting)
Holly	*Ilex aquifolium*	Bush or hedge	Berries (autumn/winter) Cover for nesting	Thrushes, especially Mistle (feeding)
Honeysuckle	*Lonicera periclymenum*	Climbing plant	Flowers (summer) Berries (autumn)	Warblers, thrushes, finches
Ivy	*Hedera helix*	Climbing plant	Fruit (winter/spring)	Woodpigeon, Thrushes, Robin, warblers (eg Blackcap)
Oak	*Quercus robur*	Tree	Acorns (autumn) Insects, including caterpillars (spring/summer)	Jay, Woodpigeon, Nuthatch, woodpeckers (acorns), tits, etc (caterpillars)
Silver birch	*Betula pendula*	Tree	Insects (spring/summer) Catkins (autumn) Good for hole-nesters	Various species, including warblers, finches, Long-tailed Tit (feeding) Woodpeckers (nesting)
Teasel (or Teasle)	*Dipsacus fullonum*	Flowering plant	Seed heads (autumn)	Goldfinches
Willow	*Salix caprea* (and various non-native species)	Tree	Catkins (spring), Insects, including caterpillars (spring/summer)	Various species
NON-NATIVE PLANTS				
ENGLISH NAME(S)	SCIENTIFIC NAME(S)	TYPE OF PLANT	KEY FEATURES	TO ATTRACT
Barberry (Berberis)	*Berberis aggregata* *B. gagnepainni* *B. thunbergii* *B. wilsoniae*	Shrub	Fruits (autumn)	Various species
Cotoneaster	*Cotoneaster* (various varieties)	Shrub	Berries (autumn and winter)	Thrushes, including Redwing & Fieldfare; Waxwing
Cypresses (especially Lawson and Leyland)	*Chamaecyparis lawsoniana* *Cupressocyparis leylandii*	Coniferous tree or hedge	Cover for roosting and nesting birds	Various species, including Greenfinch, Goldcrest, Collared Dove & Woodpigeon
Firethorn or Pyracantha	*Pyracantha* (various species)	Shrub	Berries (autumn)	Various species, including winter thrushes, Woodpigeon
Forsythia	*Forsythia* (various species)	Bush or hedge	Buds (early spring)	Bullfinch
Flowering nutmeg or Himalayan honeysuckle	*Leycesteria formosa*	Shrub	Fruit (autumn)	Various species, including tits, thrushes, finches & warblers
Honesty	*Lunaria biennis*	Flowering plant	Seeds (autumn)	Finches, especially Bullfinch
Sunflower	*Helianthus annuus*	Flowering plant	Seeds (autumn)	Finches
Wisteria	*Wisteria sinensis*	Climbing plant	Insects (spring/summer) Cover for nesting	Warblers, flycatchers (feeding) Various species (nesting)
Yew	*Taxus baccata*	Tree or hedge	Fruit (mid-summer) Cover for nesting	Thrushes, especially Mistle (feeding) Various species, including Wren (nesting)

WATCHING AND RECORDING GARDEN BIRDS

WATCHING

There may still be a little way to go before you have created the ideal habitat, but already birds are beginning to appear. To enjoy them even more, you should invest in a decent pair of binoculars for close-up views and a notebook to record your sightings (see below).

Nothing makes more difference to the pleasure of watching birds than using binoculars. You don't need to spend a fortune, but you should be willing to invest a reasonable sum to get a pair that will give you a lifetime's entertainment. Avoid high-street retailers, and go to a specialist optical equipment retailer (advertised in all the major bird magazines). Explain what you want the binoculars for, and how much you're prepared to spend. Between £80 and £150 should buy you something reliable, sturdy and optically good.

Once you have bought your binoculars, keep them somewhere you can lay your hands on them immediately: there is little use in having an expensive pair of binoculars for birdwatching if, by the time you've found them, the bird has flown away.

Getting close-up views is a good start, but you still need to know what species you're looking at. To identify the birds visiting your garden, use Part Two of this book: the Directory of Garden Birds. You may also want to purchase a field guide, although beware those that cover a very wide area, or show several hundred different species, as these can be confusing for a beginner.

RECORDING

Once you have your binoculars, now is the time to think about keeping a record of the different species that come to visit your garden.

There are a number of good reasons to keep a record of birds in your garden. First, it's fun! Making a simple 'garden list' of the various different species is a good start, but ideally you should also keep more detailed records. These should include:

- the number of individuals of each species;
- dates and times of visits;
- what the birds are doing: e.g. feeding, bathing;
- types of food taken;
- notes of any unusual or interesting behaviour: e.g. fighting, courtship;
- description of any birds you can't identify.

You may make this record as detailed or concise as you like, but it must be accurate and kept up-to-date. Later, it will be fascinating to re-read your old records and to note which species have become more common, which have disappeared completely, and with luck, some new arrivals.

CREATING A 'WILDLIFE GARDEN'

In one sense, any garden in which the owner has taken the trouble to provide plants, food and nesting sites for birds falls into the category of a 'wildlife garden'.

However, this term is usually reserved for a garden which has been specifically designed to attract the widest possible variety of insect, bird and mammal life, by duplicating in miniature the natural environment of habitats like woodland, wetland and hay-meadows. Most wildlife gardeners also avoid using pesticides and other chemicals, preferring to use natural methods of pest control where possible.

One of the first and best-known wildlife gardeners is the academic, writer and broadcaster Chris Baines. Chris first came to fame during the mid-1980s, when a BBC documentary, 'Blue Tits and Bumblebees', revealed how he transformed his own garden on the outskirts of Birmingham into a veritable wildlife paradise.

Since then, he has written several books on the subject, the best-known of which is *How to Make a Wildlife Garden* (see page 156). If you are keen to explore this subject further, and turn your lawn into a hay meadow, I would highly recommend this book!

Letting part of your garden grow wild, so that there are plenty of native plants, will attract birds such as this Goldcrest.

If you enjoy photography, why not make a visual record of your garden birds? By using a small, portable hide, or sitting quietly in one corner of the garden, you should be able to get spectacular close-up shots. However, make sure you do not disturb feeding or nesting birds, as this may reduce their chances of survival or breeding success.

THE GARDEN BIRDWATCH SURVEY

You may be happy to keep records purely for your own personal enjoyment, but with a little extra effort you can make a valuable contribution to the conservation of British garden birds.

For more than a quarter of a century, members of the British Trust for Ornithology (BTO) have been surveying garden birds. In 1995 the BTO launched a new survey, which they called the Garden BirdWatch. This has now become the largest year-round survey of birds in the British Isles, with more than six thousand active participants up and down the country.

Members fill in the details of birds visiting their garden once a week, and the data is then analysed back at BTO headquarters to produce detailed statistics on the fortunes of our garden birds.

Since the survey began, it has already produced some fascinating results. Top of the first 'hit parade' of garden birds was the Blue Tit, and since then this favourite species has never been outside the top three (see Garden Birdwatch chart below). Other findings have included

rises in the presence of some of the relatively uncommon garden species, such as the Long-tailed Tit and the Goldfinch. There have also been notable seasonal variations in the numbers of birds reported. These are related to unusual weather conditions, such as drought in summer and prolonged cold spells in recent winters.

To participate in the Garden BirdWatch survey, contact the BTO (see page 157 for details). There is a registration fee of £10 to be paid as a contribution towards administration costs, but in return, members get discounts on food for wild birds. They also receive a quarterly magazine, *The Bird Table*, which is full of informative articles and the latest survey results. The BTO are especially keen to hear from people with small, urban gardens, and also gardens of any type in northern England, Wales, Scotland and Ireland.

Spend time watching the birds in your garden, and you will see some fascinating behaviour. These Great Tits and Blue Tit are squabbling among themselves over who should feed on the peanuts.

GARDEN BIRDWATCH

PERIOD	1	2	3	4	5	6	7	8	9	10
AUTUMN 94	Blue Tit	Blackbird	Robin	House Sparrow	Great Tit	Dunnock	Starling	Chaffinch	Greenfinch	Collared Dove
WINTER 95	Blackbird	Blue Tit	Robin	House Sparrow	Chaffinch	Great Tit	Dunnock	Starling	Greenfinch	Collared Dove
SPRING 95	Blackbird	House Sparrow	Blue Tit	Starling	Greenfinch	Collared Dove	Robin	Great Tit	Chaffinch	Dunnock
SUMMER 95	Blue Tit	Blackbird	House Sparrow	Robin	Great Tit	Collared Dove	Greenfinch	Dunnock	Starling	Chaffinch
AUTUMN 95	Blue Tit	Robin	Blackbird	House Sparrow	Great Tit	Dunnock	Starling	Greenfinch	Collared Dove	Chaffinch
WINTER 96	Blackbird	Blue Tit	Robin	House Sparrow	Dunnock	Chaffinch	Starling	Great Tit	Greenfinch	Collared Dove
SPRING 96	Blackbird	Blue Tit	House Sparrow	Starling	Greenfinch	Robin	Collared Dove	Dunnock	Chaffinch	Great Tit
SUMMER 96	Blue Tit	Blackbird	House Sparrow	Collared Dove	Great Tit	Robin	Greenfinch	Dunnock	Chaffinch	Starling
AUTUMN 96	Blue Tit	Robin	Blackbird	Great Tit	House Sparrow	Chaffinch	Dunnock	Collared Dove	Greenfinch	Starling

2

FEEDING GARDEN BIRDS

I guess that in every winter now, in every country in Europe, in every state in North America, in Japan, and in some other countries of the southern hemisphere, hundreds of tons of good and fairly expensive food will be given to the wild birds.

JAMES FISHER, *THE SHELL BIRD BOOK*

FEEDING GARDEN BIRDS

Once upon a time, feeding garden birds was very simple: you just chucked a few scraps of stale bread onto the lawn and waited for the birds to arrive. Today, the situation has changed completely. Feeding garden birds is a multi-million pound industry. An extraordinary range of feeders and feeding stations now dispense gourmet foods that would do justice to a Cordon Bleu chef.

Each year, we in the United Kingdom provide an estimated fifteen thousand tonnes of peanuts for birds – more than thirty billion nuts, or more than eight hundred lorryloads. We haven't yet reached the level of interest found in the United States, where a staggering two billion dollars is spent on feeding birds every year.

Artificial bird feeders are an essential addition to any garden, especially during the winter, when they provide a valuable supplement to the birds' natural diet.

WHY FEED GARDEN BIRDS?

Feeding garden birds is one of our most popular pastimes: a recent national survey by the RSPB revealed that two out of three people regularly put out food for birds in winter. But why go to so much time, trouble and expense to provide food for wild creatures? Can't they fend for themselves?

Perhaps the most obvious reason for feeding the birds is that without our help, many simply would not survive the winter. Birds compete among themselves to find food, to provide energy. During spells of ice and snow, when food resources dwindle, birds will starve unless we provide extra supplies of food.

Small birds in particular need to obtain large quantities of food on a regular basis: in the cold winter months a bird like the Blue Tit or Robin must eat between one-quarter and one-third of its body weight every single day.

Moreover, the wholesale destruction of habitat in our countryside means that many naturally occurring foods, such as our native plants and insects, are now much more scarce than before. This is especially

Feeding birds in winter can help declining species, such as the Tree Sparrow, survive.

true during the breeding season, when there are hungry mouths to feed. Without extra food, breeding success would be reduced, and eventually, populations would begin to decline.

In recent years, some ornithologists have argued that by providing such large quantities of high-quality, 'artificial' food for birds, we may in some way be upsetting the balance of nature, and favouring common garden birds at the expense of the birds in woodland and farmland habitats.

However, most people now agree that feeding garden birds has a beneficial effect on bird populations, especially those in urban and suburban areas, where natural food is particularly scarce.

How to Feed Garden Birds

You can provide food for garden birds in two ways:

● by planting trees, bushes and shrubs which produce fruits or berries, or which attract insects *(see* Chapter 1, Planning the Garden, page 12);
● by providing food yourself, such as kitchen scraps, seeds and peanuts.

There are a few basic rules of garden bird feeding:

1. Always provide a variety of different foods, arranged at different levels, to attract different species.
2. Feed the birds regularly – once birds have been attracted to your garden by the provision of food, don't suddenly let them down by withdrawing the supply.

3. Keep your bird table and feeders well-stocked, clean and tidy to reduce the chance of disease, and to avoid attracting unwelcome pests such as rats and mice.
4. Start by providing a range of basic foods to suit your budget; then gradually build up to provide a more complex range of items.
5. Buy the food from approved dealers or from the RSPB. Whatever you do, avoid the 'birdseed' sold in pet shops and supermarkets. It may be unsuitable for wild birds.

CENTRE STAGE: THE BIRD TABLE

For many people, the bird table is the start and finish of garden bird feeding, a means of attracting a reasonable range of species for the minimum amount of effort. For others, it leads to more interesting and ambitious projects, eventually becoming the centrepiece of a full-scale 'service station' for the birds.

The popularity of bird tables for their owners and the birds is easy to explain. A bird table enables you to provide a variety of foodstuffs, gives shelter to feeding birds in bad weather, stops food going bad, and deters at least some of the unwelcome visitors to your garden.

A bird table is the centrepiece of any bird-friendly garden. The sloping roof keeps the food dry.

Bird tables come in all shapes and sizes – but if you don't like the designs in the shops, why not make your own?

THE BIRD TABLE DILEMMA: TO BUY OR TO MAKE?

Should you purchase one of the many different types of bird table on sale or have a go at making one yourself? That will depend on your budget and DIY ability, but whichever you choose, there are several important things to remember:

1. Avoid the ornamental bird tables found at many garden centres. Thatched roofs may look pretty, but are not very practical, and may add to the cost.
2. Buy only from a reputable supplier, such as the RSPB or one of the specialist companies listed under Useful Addresses (see page 157). This will guarantee that the table you buy has been thoroughly tested on birds and, where necessary, modified to suit them.
3. Start with something relatively simple. Bird table prices start at around £20 (often requiring basic self-assembly and a post on which to mount the table). You can pay well over £100 for the latest hi-tech, squirrel-proof design, but it is best to start with a basic model.
4. Make sure the pole is thick and sturdy enough to support the weight of the table, and that it will stand up to high winds. Either mount the pole into the ground, making sure you dig deep enough to keep it stable, or choose a pole with a sturdy base.
5. Site your bird table carefully. It should be in the open, not too close to bushes, trees or fences, to make sure that cats can't take advantage of a free lunch. On the other hand, if it is too far away from a suitable perch, the birds will not be able to reach the table easily. Experiment with two or three locations until you find the ideal one.
6. If you decide to make your own bird table, use plans approved by the RSPB, or follow the instructions below.

MAKING YOUR OWN BIRD TABLE

Making a bird table is easier than you think. After all, it doesn't have to look pretty: it just has to be large and sturdy enough to hold the food and allow the birds to feed comfortably.

This design is for the simplest possible table, without a roof. If you decide to add a roof, make it slope and overlap the table edges by a couple of centimetres, so that water running off it cannot fall on to the table and contaminate the food.

If you prefer you can hang your table from a branch, or even mount it on a window ledge, using hooks and wire, or chain.

To make a bird table, you will need the following:

- A **flat piece of wood** for the base (preferably plywood, obtainable from any timber supplier), about 0.5–1 cm (½ in) thick, 30–40 cm (12–15 in) wide and 50–60 cm (20–24 in) long.
- 150–200 cm (60–80 in) **length of wood or doweling**, around 0.5–1 cm (½ in) square, for the rim (to prevent food falling off the table).
- a **sturdy wooden post**, around 8–10 cm (3½–4 in) square, and between 120–180 cm (48–72 in) long (if you are making a base) or 30 cm (12 in) longer if you plan to mount the pole in the ground.
- **eight blocks of wood**, around 6–8 cm (2½–3 in) square and 30–40 cm (12–14 in) long, for the base (if required).
- **four metal angle brackets** (obtainable from DIY stores), to fix the pole to the bottom of the table.

- a selection of **wood screws** of different lengths.
- **Tools:** an electric drill, screwdriver, saw, large mallet.
- Wood glue and sandpaper.

How to assemble the bird table:

1. Measure and cut the wood or doweling strips to length, allowing a small gap in each corner to let water drain off.
2. Drill two or three small holes along each edge of the base.
3. Using a waterproof wood glue or paste, stick the wood strips along all four sides of the base, remembering to allow a small gap in each corner. Allow to dry.
4. For extra strength, attach screws through each of the holes.
5. Using sandpaper, smooth off any sharp corners to avoid injury to the birds.
6. If you are making a base, cut four blocks of wood to act as the feet, and attach them to the bottom of the pole using glue and screws. For extra strength, add four braces.
7. Place the pole on the underside of the table and mark where to attach the angle brackets. Drill small holes and attach the brackets using wood screws. (NB: If your table is to be mounted in a hole in the ground, do this afterwards).
8. If you plan to mount the pole in the ground, dig a hole slightly smaller than the diameter of the pole and about 20 cm deep. Then using a large mallet, drive the pole into the hole to a depth of around 30 cm. Make sure it is secure.
9. As a final touch, make sure you coat the exposed surface with a clear wood preservative, letting it dry thoroughly before the birds use the table.

Food for Bird Tables

You have begged, borrowed, bought or made your bird table and set it up in the garden. Now you need to put some food on it. Bird tables are designed to hold all kinds of different foods: anything from a crust of bread to leftovers from a meal. Avoid very hard or stale foods, however, as these may cause a bird to choke, or give digestive problems. You should also avoid whole peanuts, as these are too large for birds to eat easily, and may cause choking. Either place peanuts in feeders *(see below),* or put out small peanut granules.

Suitable food for bird tables includes the following:

- **bread:** the staple diet of many garden birds. Make sure you don't put out more than the birds can eat in a day. If the bread is stale, soak it first, or crumble into pieces. Will attract Starlings and House Sparrows.

A mixture of foodstuffs such as bread, cooked rice and lentils provide an excellent supplementary diet for a wide variety of bird species.

- **dried fruit** (raisins, sultanas, etc) This is one of the very best kinds of food for birds: as it has a very high energy content. It is most likely to attract Blackbirds, thrushes and Robins. You may want to soak it first to make it easier for the birds to digest.

Apples are especially popular with larger birds such as the Blackbird, and other species of thrush including the wintering Fieldfare and Redwing.

- **fresh fruit:** apples are very popular, especially among thrushes and Blackbirds, although they usually prefer to feed on the ground. Bits of orange, grapes, etc are also very welcome!
- **bacon:** avoid very salty bacon; otherwise excellent. You can either hang it up, or chop it to attract birds like Robins and tits.
- **grated cheese:** like bacon, its high fat content provides essential energy, especially in cold weather. Very popular with Robins.
- **beef or lamb suet:** an excellent and cheap way of providing high-energy fat, also very valuable in cold weather. Very popular with tits, and may also attract Great Spotted Woodpeckers.
- **pet food:** tinned dog or cat food is ideal, as it is cheap and nutritious! However, avoid dog biscuits, as they are too hard for the birds. Especially popular with Starlings.

- **cooked rice:** brown or white rice is a popular food, although be careful not to add salt, as this may be harmful. Also very popular with Starlings.
- **porridge oats or coarse oatmeal:** popular with many species, including Chaffinches and, during the winter in some areas, Bramblings.
- **cooked potatoes:** either baked, boiled, roasted or mashed. Popular with Starlings.
- **coconut:** half a coconut hanging from the base of the bird table will attract acrobatic Blue and Great Tits, giving hours of enjoyment as you watch their antics. However, never give desiccated coconut as it may swell up inside the bird's stomach and cause injury or death.

Many people hang other kinds of bird feeders from bird tables, using small brass hooks. However, bear in mind that too many feeders may cause congestion, so might be

Peanut feeders are cheap, simple to use, and will provide hours of entertainment as you watch the antics of feeding Blue Tits.

better placed elsewhere to attract shy birds that prefer not to visit a crowded bird table.

BASIC FEEDERS AND FOODS

FEEDERS

As well as a bird table, it's well worth providing some basic feeders. Bird feeders come in all shapes, sizes and colours, with red being especially popular amongst feeding birds. They range in price from £5 or so for a basic peanut feeder or seed dispenser, to well over £100 for huge, multi-purpose feeding-stations that look like something out of a sci-fi film!

1. Basic peanut feeders

No garden should be without at least one basic peanut feeder. These are usually made out of wire mesh, with a plastic or metal base and cover, which is removable to

---

DISEASE AT BIRD TABLES

Because bird tables attract a large number of different birds, food can easily become contaminated, leading to the possibility of diseases such as salmonella poisoning. Birds that feed in flocks, such as Greenfinches and House Sparrows, appear to be particularly vulnerable.

Signs that your garden birds may be suffering from disease include an abnormally large number of dead birds, or birds appearing weak or ill.

You can reduce the chances of disease on your bird table by taking some simple precautions. First, never put mouldy food out on a bird table. Second, always remove unused food, as it may attract rats or mice. Third, keep the table and the surrounding area clean – if necessary by using a mild solution of Jeyes Fluid and a scrubbing brush! Whatever you do, make sure that you rinse the table very carefully to remove all traces of the chemical before further use.

If you want to find out more, there is an information leaflet available: 'Diseases of Garden Birds – Minimising the Risks'. To obtain a free copy, send a stamped addressed envelope to: James Kirkwood, Universities Federation for Animal Welfare, 8 Hamilton Close, South Mimms, Potters Bar, Herts EN6 3QD. You can also report any suspected cases of disease to the same address.

allow you to refill when empty. They are usually hung from a post, tree or bird table by means of a wire, but can also be mounted on a pole. Some models even come with rubber stickers on the side to attach to a window – perfect for close-up views!

Peanut feeders range in size from around 12.5 cm (5 in) long, designed for one or two birds at a time, to around 30 cm (12 in) long, which will support half a dozen or more birds feeding at the same time.

2. Basic seed feeders

These are similar in shape to peanut feeders, and also have a plastic or metal base and cover, but are made from clear polycarbonate tubing. There are usually between two and six small openings to allow the birds to get to the contents. Each opening normally has a small perch to allow the birds to feed more easily.

Seed feeders range in size from around 20 cm (8 in) to more than 1m (40 in) long, holding more than a kilogram of food!

3. Squirrel-proof nut and seed feeders

Squirrels can be a real problem in some areas, since they not only steal the birds' food but they damage their feeders, too (see Chapter 5, Pests, Predators & Other Hazards, page 64). So one company has designed a range of squirrel-proof feeders. These are basically a standard nut or seed feeder enclosed in a sturdy wire cage, which allows the birds access while keeping squirrels out. Although these are more expensive than basic feeders, they are well worth considering, especially if squirrels regularly visit your garden.

If you have a problem with Grey Squirrels, try installing a squirrel-proof feeder such as this one. The wire cage lets the birds through, but keeps the squirrels out.

FOODS

Peanuts

Peanuts are a popular food with many species of garden birds, especially tits, Greenfinches and sparrows. Because they have a very high oil and protein content, peanuts are one of the healthiest and most energy-efficient

Peanuts are the staple diet of many garden birds, especially tits, finches and sparrows. Make sure you put them in a suitable feeder, so that small birds cannot choke on whole nuts.

foods available to birds. Peanuts are not nuts at all, but pulses, related to the bean family. They originally came from South America, but they are grown today in many sub-tropical areas of the world, such as Africa, Asia and the USA.

A few years ago there were a number of incidents of peanuts poisoning wild birds. These were caused by a chemical known as aflatoxin, from a fungus which is produced when nuts get damp. Aflatoxin poisons birds by damaging their liver and immune system, and is known to have caused a number of deaths.

To prevent this, the wild birdfood trade, along with the RSPB and BTO, set up the Birdfood Standards Association (BSA), to campaign for safer peanuts. Fortunately, this seems to have worked, and peanuts on sale by reputable suppliers are now all free from aflatoxin.

It is usually cheaper to buy your peanuts in bulk: prices range from around £8–10 for 4 kg (8.8 lb), which works out at £2–2.50 per kg (2.2 lb); to £60–70 for 50 kg (110 lb), or £1.20–1.40 per kg (2.2 lb). However, never buy too many in one go, as if kept for too long, peanuts may go mouldy. Always store them in a cool, dry place, and in a sturdy bag or box to keep away rodents.

Seeds and grains

Seeds are the staple diet of many species of garden birds, including tits, finches, sparrows and pigeons, while grains are the winter diet of many woodland and farmland species. Like peanuts, they provide essential oils and vitamins, and maximize

Seeds provide birds with valuable energy. They are particularly popular with finches, sparrows and buntings.

Black sunflower seeds have proved to be very popular with a wide variety of garden birds, especially finches.

the energy available for the minimum feeding effort. The most popular varieties of seeds and grains are sunflower seeds, oatmeal, millet, wheat and maize, but all kinds of more unusual seeds, such as niger (a small variety of sunflower) are now available and will attract specialized feeders such as Goldfinches. Not all seeds are suitable all year round, and some suppliers produce a variety of seeds to suit summer and winter feeding.

Seeds and grains vary in price, depending on the type of seed and the amount required. As with peanuts, bulk buying is more economical, and if stored in clean, dry, cool conditions most seeds will keep for several months.

Prices for basic sunflower seeds range from around £6 for 4 kg (8.8 lb), which works out at £1.50 per kg (2.2 lb), to £50 for 50 kg (110 lb), or £1 per kg (2.2 lb). More exotic seeds, such as niger, the tiny seed of thistles, should cost around £1.50–£2.50 per kg (2.2 lb).

Until recently House Sparrows rarely visited artificial seed feeders. Today, however, they are a common sight, often displacing less aggressive species.

SPECIALIZED FOODS

Nuts and seeds are the basic foodstuffs for birds, but if you want to attract an even wider variety of species, you may want to branch out into more exotic foods. These come in a variety of shapes, sizes and prices – and the contents may be offputting if you are at all squeamish. Bear in mind, however, that it is for a good cause, and will be very popular with the birds.

Specialized fat products

My grandmother always used to put out beef suet for the birds. Saturated fats like this are ideal, as they provide essential energy and vitamins while remaining relatively hard and solid, so avoiding mess.

Nowadays, as our diets have become healthier, and we try to avoid saturated fats, we may not have anything suitable. Fortunately, you can now buy a whole range of fat products specially designed for feeding garden birds.

The simplest of these are basic food bars: a combination of animal fats, seeds and sometimes insects, which can be hung up from a bird table or a branch of a tree. They are especially popular with smaller birds such as Blue, Great and Coal Tits, Greenfinch and Chaffinch, and Robin, and may also attract more unusual visitors to your garden, such as Treecreeper, Goldcrest and Blackcap. Food bars cost around £3 to £5, depending on size and weight.

If you don't want to go to that expense, why not make your own? First, melt the suet in a saucepan, adding three times the same weight of seed to absorb the fat and give the mixture solidity. Then place the mixture into a mould, and put it in the fridge to harden. After an hour or so, insert a thick piece of wire to enable you to hang it up. When completely solid (usually after 2–3 hours), hang it on a branch or bird table and wait for the birds.

A word of warning – make sure you take care when mixing the hot fat, especially if children are helping.

Live food

Not all birds feed on nuts, seeds and grains. Birds such as warblers, flycatchers and robins are insect-eaters, and until

You can buy specially-designed food bars, containing a mixture of fat, seeds and sometimes even insects, designed to attract discerning feeders such as the Blackcap.

recently have been difficult to attract to feeding-stations and bird tables.

Now, however, things are changing, and to make the most of your feeding you really need to add live food to the menu!

Many people are put off the idea of live food, with visions of maggots, worms and blowflies running riot in our houses and gardens. In fact, live food is clean and hygienic so that you can even keep it in your fridge!

The best live foods to choose are mealworms and waxworms. Neither are actually worms, but the larvae of insects: the

Tit bells, filled with fat for birds like this Great Tit, are popular additions to your feeding-station, and will provide many hours of entertainment for you and the birds.

Meal Beetle and Wax Moth respectively. These can be bought from specialist dealers.

If kept in a cool place such as a garden shed or garage, mealworms will last for two to three months, while waxworms keep for three to four weeks. Avoid maggots, as these are believed to cause salmonella in birds.

Put live food in a smooth-sided bowl (to prevent escape!), and place it either on the ground, bird table or on a wall or rockery where the birds can easily see it. All sorts of birds may come to investigate, including Robins, Dunnocks, sparrows, tits, warblers and even Jays. Live food is also very popular with Starling flocks. But beware! If they become regular visitors you may soon find yourself bankrupt.

Live food is particularly valuable at certain times of year: during the breeding season, when birds need all the help they can get to feed hungry young; and during hard winter weather, snow or heavy rain, when other sources of food may be hard to come by.

Ground-feeding Birds and Ways to Feed Them

Many birds, such as doves and pigeons, thrushes, buntings, Robins and Dunnocks, are basically ground feeders. Others, such as Starling, Chaffinch and Brambling, often prefer to feed on the ground too.

Providing food for these species takes a bit of thought: just scattering scraps from the kitchen may attract unwelcome visitors such as rats or mice, especially if food is left out overnight.

Follow these few basic rules:

• place food on blocks of wood, so that it is easy to see how much is left at the end of the day.
• clear up food each evening, especially during warm weather, when it may rot.
• try to provide a variety of food, such as apples (a great favourite with winter thrushes), dried fruit, and to attract Starlings, cooked potatoes and cooked rice.

Summer Feeding

One of the current controversies about garden birds is whether or not you should continue to feed them during the spring and summer months, the time when they are raising their young.

Until recently, the vast majority of people fed birds only during the winter, when they seem to need food the most. As well as the belief that birds could get all they needed in spring and summer from natural food sources, there was also a fear that young birds might choke on unsuitable food such as peanuts.

However, in the last year or two, the BTO in particular, aided by a leading wild birdfood supplier, has begun to promote summer feeding.

Baby birds need a large supply of invertebrates such as caterpillars, grubs and flies. However, these are in short supply in most gardens, owing to the lack of mature trees such as oaks, and are especially scarce at the start of the breeding season. The parent birds may therefore have to choose between feeding themselves or their young.

So by providing seeds and peanuts for birds, the

Live mealworms can be put out to provide a juicy alternative meal for many birds, such as this Blue Tit.

argument goes, we are giving the adults a steady, reliable food supply, enabling them to give all the natural food they can to their young.

Not everybody agrees with this, and there have been fears that adults will continue to feed peanuts to young, causing them to choke. So the BTO has drawn up a code of conduct on feeding outside the winter season:

● continue to provide food throughout the spring and summer, but vary the diet to include more live food if possible.
● never put out whole peanuts. Instead, provide peanut granules, or use a wire mesh feeder to prevent the birds obtaining large chunks.
● reduce the amount of food you provide during the autumn (August to October), as this is the period when most natural food is available.

Recent results from the BTO's Garden BirdWatch Survey show that some species, including Great Tit, Greenfinch and Chaffinch, are present more than twice as often in gardens where birds are fed during the summer than those where they are not. Amazingly, these gardens also had more birds present during the autumn, whether or not they continued to put out food.

Feeding in Harsh Weather

Towards the end of one of the worst winters this century, the legendary 'Big Freeze' of 1962/63, the ornithologist and broadcaster James Fisher gave a chilling verdict on the state of Britain's bird population: 'It seems likely that at least half the wild birds living in this country before last Christmas are now dead'.

Although Fisher later admitted that this might have been a slight exaggeration, he probably wasn't too far off the mark. No-one knows exactly how many birds perished during that terrible winter, but the total must have run into tens of millions. Small species such as the Wren were particularly badly hit, with as much as ninety per cent of the population perishing.

During a prolonged spell of ice and snow, our gardens become a vital refuge for the birds. Pay a visit to your local wood and you'll soon discover why: natural food sources become so depleted, particularly in late winter, that there may simply be no food left for the birds.

Familiar species, such as tits, sparrows and finches, become more common as they head into towns, villages and suburbs to take advantage of the food on offer. You may also be lucky enough to get some more unusual garden visitors: perhaps woodpeckers, a Nuthatch, or winter thrushes such as Redwing and Fieldfare.

Contrary to popular belief, it is not so much the cold which kills birds in harsh winter weather, but the shortage of food. So by providing regular supplies, you can contribute to helping wild bird populations survive to breed again the following spring. The key word here is 'regular'. The worst thing you can do in harsh winter weather is interrupt the supply of food or stop feeding altogether. Another tip: during snowy weather make regular checks to ensure that the food doesn't get covered with a layer of snow. Finally, don't forget that a regular supply of water for drinking and bathing is just as important as food (*see* Chapter 3, Water in the Garden, page 40).

CHANGES IN DIET

However, some unusual ways of feeding soon become widespread throughout the population of a particular species. For example, House Sparrows feeding from hanging bags of peanuts was hardly ever recorded a couple of decades ago, yet today it is a common sight. The same is true of the Goldfinch, which is increasingly reported as taking peanuts from hanging feeders.

Leave windfall apples on the ground, or scatter them beneath the bird table, to attract winter thrushes such as this Fieldfare.

Recent observations of birds at peanut feeders have included insect-eaters such as the Dunnock and a wintering Chiffchaff. This change of diet can probably be explained by a lack of suitable invertebrate food. In the case of the Chiffchaff, diversifying its diet may also prove to be of evolutionary advantage, enabling a higher proportion of birds to survive the British winter.

One of the great success stories of garden bird feeding in recent years has been the huge increase in the numbers of Siskins visiting gardens. Twenty-five years ago, when the BTO first surveyed garden birds, only seven per cent of gardens enjoyed visits from this delightful little finch.

Food scraps scattered on a lawn can attract unusual garden visitors such as this Moorhen. However, be sure to clean up excess food every evening, or you may attract unwelcome visitors such as rats and mice.

Today, almost two-thirds of gardens have reported Siskins. Their rise may be to do with the popularity of peanuts in red bags, which are thought to resemble giant versions of the Siskin's favourite natural food, alder cones. However, Siskins have also been helped by the spread of forestry plantations, where they prefer to nest.

TITS AND MILK BOTTLES

Without doubt, however, the most famous new development in garden bird feeding techniques occurred more than half a century ago, when it was first discovered that Blue Tits could open the tops of milk bottles to get at the contents.

The habit spread so rapidly that some observers concluded that it was being passed on genetically, or even by telepathy. In fact, it was simply the case that once the habit was widely publicized, people throughout the country began to realize the cause of the damage to their daily pinta.

The tits' method is simple but effective. The bird lands on the top of the bottle, and pecks away at the foil top until it has made a hole large enough to poke its head inside. Tits aren't the only birds to have developed this habit: Magpies have also been observed breaking into milk bottles. Despite appearances, the birds are not in fact stealing the milk, but the cream. This is because milk may cause diarrhoea in birds, while the full-fat content of cream is much easier to digest – and more nutritious and energy-efficient, too.

With the invention of the cardboard carton, the recent decline in doorstep milk deliveries and the rise in popularity of skimmed and semi-skimmed milk, the days of doorstep robbery may be coming to an end, to the relief of many householders. However, in 1993 a Carrion Crow in Fife was observed gaining access to a milk carton, so perhaps the birds will continue to adapt to new designs for milk containers made from different materials, such as plastics.

UNUSUAL FOODS & FEEDING BEHAVIOUR

Most birds have a staple diet of foods which they prefer to eat. Some have a highly specialized diet, such as the Goldfinch's preference for niger and teasel seeds. Others, like the Starling, are much more catholic in taste, feeding on a wide variety of natural foods and those provided by us.

However, from time to time birds will change their preferences, and try out something new. This may be a one-off occurrence, such as the Blackbird feeding on tadpoles at a garden pond in Gwynedd, Wales; another Blackbird, this time in Humberside, eating the contents of a discarded tub of chocolate ice-cream; or the Great Spotted Woodpecker feeding on nectar in a Norfolk garden.

3

WATER IN THE GARDEN

*A wildlife garden without a pond is like a theatre
without a stage.*

CHRIS BAINES, *HOW TO MAKE A WILDLIFE GARDEN*

WHY BIRDS NEED WATER

Water is essential for birds. As well as drinking, birds also need to bathe regularly, to keep their plumage in tip-top condition. Birds will drink or bathe from any available source of water – often taking advantage of puddles after a fall of rain. However, because natural sources of water for drinking and bathing may be far away or in short supply, it is a good idea to provide at least one regular source of water if you wish to attract birds to your garden.

WATER FOR DRINKING

Birds get most of their moisture through the food they eat, and because they do not sweat or produce urine they do not need to drink as frequently as we do.

Insect-eating species such as warblers generally need to drink less frequently than seed-eating species, because their provides more moisture. Nevertheless, most small birds need to drink at least once or twice a day.

Drinking can be hazardous, as it makes the bird vulnerable to predators, so most species have evolved a drinking method that enables them to keep a lookout. This involves taking a swift sip of water, tipping the head back to allow the water to run down the throat by force of gravity, then repeating the process until they have drunk enough.

Bathing is essential to maintain plumage in tip-top condition. Birds like this Blackbird often have a daily bath to keep their feathers clean.

BATHING

Bathing is vital for birds to keep their plumage clean and their feathers in tip-top condition. It is especially important in winter, as it allows them to fluff out their feathers properly to insulate themselves against the cold.

When bathing, most birds do not immerse themselves totally in the water, since this might cause their feathers to become waterlogged, and put them in danger from predators or from cold weather.

Instead, a bathing bird usually stands at the edge of the water, and splashes water over its plumage by shaking itself, ruffling its feathers and fluttering its wings. These activities ensure that the water covers the whole of the bird's plumage without soaking it completely.

After bathing, birds often sit out in the sun to dry off as quickly as possible. They may spend this time preening: putting their feathers back in neat order, and cleaning them to ensure that they continue to work properly.

Birds generally bathe once a day, although this varies depending on the cleanliness of the plumage and the environment in which they live. Because natural sources of water such as lakes and ponds may be some distance away, many garden birds depend on those provided by us: either in the form of bird baths or garden ponds.

Above: *Birds need to drink frequently, particularly if, like this Woodpigeon, they feed mainly on dry food such as grain or seeds.*

Left: *Water can transform a garden into a paradise for visiting birds. As well as appealing to the commoner species, you may also attract rarer visitors such as Redpolls, Hawfinches and Crossbills.*

BIRD BATHS

A bird bath may look like just any other piece of ornamental garden furniture, but it has an essential role to play in the lives of garden birds. A well-designed bird bath is a source of drinking water for birds and a place for them to bathe.

A good bird bath should have the following features:

- sturdy, simple construction, without too many fancy features;
- shallow sides, to allow birds to drink without slipping into the water;
- a rough surface on which birds can grip with their claws;
- it should not be too heavy so that you can clean and refill it with water easily.

The simplest form of bird bath is simply a large dish or a metal or plastic lid, such as a dustbin lid, placed on stones or bricks, or sunk into the ground. If you use a dish or any other container, choose one that has a shallow gradient, which will enable different sized birds to bathe at different depths.

You can buy bird baths from garden centres, the RSPB and specialist suppliers (see Useful Addresses page 157). It is inadvisable to buy some of the fancier models sold in garden centres – they may look attractive, but are often designed to appeal more to the human eye than to birds.

Bird baths come in all shapes and sizes, and at prices ranging from around £10. They may be made from stone, fibreglass, ceramics or plastic, and there is one model on sale that uses solar energy to prevent the water from freezing in winter.

A bird bath is an attractive garden ornament, but also valuable for the birds. This Feral Pigeon is having a quick bathe.

Once your bird bath is in position, it shouldn't take long for the birds to discover it, and you'll soon be getting regular visits from birds eager to have a drink and a bathe. Sociable birds like Starlings may come in a flock, resulting in pushing, shoving and all sorts of squabbles – adding to your entertainment as you watch their antics.

Remember, make sure that you change the water regularly, to avoid the build-up of germs or bacteria that may cause disease. Birds often drink straight after feeding, and deposit bits and pieces of uneaten food, which can also pollute the water. Every week or so, give your bird bath a thorough clean. You can use household cleaners such as bleach, but do make sure that you rinse the bath thoroughly after cleaning to remove any traces of chemicals.

Ultimately, a bird bath is a welcome addition to any garden – providing an attractive centrepiece as well as an essential service for the birds.

Watching the antics of bathing birds can be instructive and fascinating, as well as great fun! This flock of adult and juvenile Starlings are enjoying their daily bath.

Garden Ponds

If you really want to provide a five-star service for the birds, and attract a wider variety of unusual visitors to your garden, you need to go the whole hog and construct a garden pond.

A pond can benefit birds and the owners of gardens in the following ways:

- it provides clean, oxygenated water for birds to drink;
- it provides a safe, accessible place for them to bathe;
- it attracts insects and other invertebrates, which are a natural food source;
- it may attract water-loving birds such as a Heron or a Kingfisher;
- it looks good, and provides hours of entertainment.

It is commonly thought that only a large garden can accommodate a pond, but this is not true. A pond may be as small as two square metres (twenty square feet) – or as large as you have room for, and can afford.

Planning a Garden Pond

Start by deciding whether you really want a pond in your garden. A great deal of work is involved in constructing a pond, and as much for the sake of your garden's appearance as for the birds, you will have to be prepared to carry out regular maintenance work.

Assuming you decide to go ahead, the major decisions to be made at the planning stage are where to put your pond and how big it should be.

Siting a pond is critical to its success. You should consider the following factors:

1. A pond should be in sight of a window so that you can watch birds that come to it to drink and to bathe.
2. Choose a site that is fairly warm and sunny and that has at least a little vegetation growing around it. Ideally, it should face a southerly to westerly direction.
3. Try to find the lowest point of your garden, as a pond sited there will collect rainwater more easily than a pond positioned high up a slope.

A pond can transform your garden into a wildlife haven, attracting insects and frogs as well as a multitude of birds.

A garden pond doesn't have to be huge: even the smallest pond will help attract birds to your garden, and provide a place to drink and bathe.

4. Avoid siting your pond under large, overhanging trees, as these block out the sunlight and cause problems with fallen leaves in autumn.

5. Plan the shape of your pond. Avoid straight, regular sides, instead going for a smooth, curved shape. Before you begin making your pond, mark out the shape with a length of rope, a hosepipe or bamboo poles placed upright in the ground. This will help you to visualize what the pond will look like when finished.

EQUIPMENT

Before you start, you will need:

● a **sharp spade**, to dig your hole, and a **wheelbarrow,** to carry away the soil.

● **rope**, a length of **hose,** or **bamboo poles** to mark out the shape of the pond.

● a **tape measure** to measure the maximum length, width and depth, and a calculator, to work out the size of lining you will need.

● a **lining**. Hard plastic shells are not very suitable for wildlife, as their sides are usually far too steep. Instead, go for a flexible pond liner, preferably made from butyl rubber – it may be a little more expensive than PVC, but it will last many times longer. Black is the best colour, as

it reduces growth of algae and provides better reflections. Linings are obtainable from most garden centres and specialist aquatic suppliers.

● **old blanket, piece of carpet** or **underlay**, to place under the lining to make a smooth surface for the pond liner to rest on.

● **sharp knife** or **scissors** to cut the lining to size and shape.

● **spirit level** to check that the edges are level all round.

● **bricks, stones** or **pieces of turf** to hold the lining in position and hide its edges.

● **sand** or **gravel** to cover the lining once it is in position.

MAKING A GARDEN POND

1. Dig a hole, starting in the centre and working out to the edges. You should dig about 15 cm (6 in) deeper than your desired final depth to allow room for the underlay and lining. So for a pond ranging in depth from 10–20 cm (4–8 in) deep at the sides, to 50–75 cm (20–30 in) at the centre, you need to dig a hole ranging from 25–35 cm (10–14 in) to 65–90 cm (26–36 in) deep.

2. Smooth out the surface of the earth, removing any sharp objects such as rocks, stones or glass, which might puncture the lining. Add a layer of sand.

3. Lay the piece of carpet or blanket into the hole.

4. Lay the lining on top. Do not stretch it too much as it will expand when filled with water. Make sure it overlaps all edges, then weigh it down with stones, bricks or turf.

5. Add a thin layer of sand or gravel all over the lining.

6. Fill the pond very gradually, using a garden hose, making sure you do not disturb the sand or gravel at the bottom. As the water fills, the lining will expand and stretch. Make sure all the edges are still even.

7. Add a layer of sand around the edge, together with more rocks, stones or turf, if necessary.

STOCKING A GARDEN POND

PLANTS

There are two ways of stocking a garden pond: the slow, cheap and easy way, and the quick and expensive way. The slow, cheap and easy way is to borrow a bucket full of water from the pond of a friend or neighbour, pour it in, and wait for Nature to do the rest. After a month or so, all kinds of insects and other creatures will have discovered your pond. Seeds will germinate, and by the end of a year you will have a ready-made little wetland of your own.

The quick way is to give nature a helping hand by stocking the pond with a variety of suitable plants. These are readily available from garden centres and aquatic specialists. Stocking a pond is a job that is best carried out during late winter or early spring.

Make a point of choosing native plants, as many introduced exotics can quickly overrun their native counterparts. Also, try to select a variety of submerged, floating and so-called 'emergent' plants (having their roots in the water and their foliage in the air), such as the following species:

- **Submerged:** Water-milfoil *Myriophyllum,* curled pondweed *Potamogeton crispus,* hornwort *Ceratophyllum,* and water starwort *Callitriche.*
- **Floating:** White water-lily *Nymphaea alba,* ivy-leaved duckweed *Lemna trisulca.*
- **Emergent:** Yellow iris *Iris pseudacorus,* meadowsweet *Filipendula ulmaria,* purple loosestrife *Lythrum salicaria,* rushes *Juncus,* sedges *Carex,* greater spearwort *Ranunculus lingua,* water mint *Mentha aquatica,* water forget-me-not

It is essential to have a wide variety of aquatic plants around the edges of your pond, to support insects and their larvae.

Myosotis scorpioides. Other good pond plants include water plantain *Alisma plantagoaquatica,* lesser spearwort *Ranunculus flammula,* lesser reedmace *Typha latifolia,* and bog bean *Menyanthes trifoliata.*

Always bear in mind that it is illegal to remove any plant from the wild, however common it appears, and however pretty it looks.

OTHER ANIMAL LIFE

Whichever method you use to stock your pond, after a short time you will discover that your pond is full of life, although much of it will be almost too small to be seen

Insects like this pond skater are a sign of a healthy pond, full of suitable food for birds.

A newly constructed garden pond will soon attract frogs, providing a home for them to lay their spawn.

without the aid of a microscope. The larger invertebrates may include water beetles and water snails. You may also find the pond attracts larger creatures such as frogs, toads and newts. These should be encouraged, especially if they stay to breed, as their natural habitat is disappearing fast, and they need all the help they can get. If you don't get any frogs, try transplanting a jar of frogspawn from a nearby pond.

The four-spotted Chaser (Libellula quadrimaculata) is a regular visitor to the garden ponds of north-west Europe.

You can put fish in your pond, but larger, more exotic specimens are best avoided as they tend to prey on everything else. Besides, you'll only lose them to a passing heron. Far better to have a few minnows or sticklebacks.

Finally, if your pond is large enough, you may be lucky enough to attract a passing dragonfly or two. Dragonflies come in all kinds of varieties, and many are an attractive addition to a garden pond.

To breed, dragonflies need a fairly large pond, with shallow water in which to lay their eggs and for their larvae to feed, and emergent plants such as irises for the newly formed adult to climb up into the open air.

With a little practice you can learn to identify the different dragonfly species almost as easily as birds and butterflies.

MAINTAINING YOUR POND

Most pond maintenance is common sense: remove autumn leaves before they cover the surface, and clear a blanket of algae from time to time. Once a year, preferably in late autumn or early winter, remove or cut back any plants threatening to take over the pond.

During hot weather or very dry conditions in summer, the level of your pond may drop an inch or two. You shouldn't need to top it up unless a drought is very prolonged.

Whatever you do, never use chemicals in your pond, even those sold for the purpose of clearing algae – they will harm the other wildlife in the pond.

KEEPING PONDS ICE-FREE IN WINTER

During harsh winter weather, getting access to a plentiful supply of water for drinking and bathing is absolutely vital for a bird's survival. Several different methods will help to keep your pond (or birdbath) ice-free:
● place a ball in the pond, and move it about as the water begins to freeze. This will keep a small area of water free of ice.
● use a kettle or saucepan of hot water to melt the ice.
● with a bird-bath, refill with warm water several times a day, or if it is made of metal, place a night light underneath.
● *never* use chemicals to melt the ice in a bird-bath or pond, as you run the risk of poisoning the birds and other wildlife living there.

Most ponds get regular visits from the local Grey Heron, who will make short work of any ornamental fish.

SAFETY AND GARDEN PONDS

One important thing to remember if you have children or grandchildren, or if young children are ever likely to visit your garden, is safety.

According to RoSPA, the Royal Society for the Prevention of Accidents, thirty children have drowned in garden ponds during the past five years. Most were toddlers, with half of them aged between one and two, and most of the rest aged between two and three. At this age, children begin to explore the world around them, but are not yet able to cope with some of the dangers. They are also likely to be fascinated by ponds, and their contents, but are unable to escape should they slip under water.

So it is important to take precautions against any potential tragedy. RoSPA actually advises parents of toddlers to drain their pond until the child is old enough to understand the potential danger. Alternatively, you can place a rigid mesh over the surface of the pond – but if you do so, make sure it is strong and rigid enough to support a child's weight.

However, bear in mind that the vast majority of these drownings did not occur at the child's home, but mainly at the homes of neighbours, friends or other relatives. So even if you don't have young children yourself, make sure others can't get access to your garden if you have a pond.

Finally, always supervise young children near water. It is so easy to lose sight of them for a minute or two – all the time needed for a child to drown, even in shallow water.

Ponds can be fascinating but dangerous places for toddlers and young children, so make sure that you follow the safety rules if children have access to your garden.

4

NESTING

*During the amorous season, such a jealousy prevails
between the male birds that they can hardly bear to
be together in the same hedge or field.*

GILBERT WHITE, *THE NATURAL HISTORY OF SELBORNE*

GARDENS AS NESTING SITES

*There are approximately 400,000 hectares (one million acres) of private garden in the
United Kingdom, and together they form a valuable refuge for our breeding birds.
Woodland species such as Robins, tits and thrushes have learned to thrive in this artificial
habitat, adapting their behaviour to suit their new environment.*

*Mature bushes and shrubs provide ideal places for many
species to build their nests and raise young.*

There are many ways in which the wildlife gardener can help protect and encourage our breeding birds:

● by planting a suitable selection of native and exotic trees, bushes and shrubs *(see* Chapter 1, Planning the Garden, page 12);
● by providing artificial **nest sites**: mainly in the form of nestboxes.

It is helpful to have a basic understanding of the breeding cycle of birds, as this will enable you to provide a wide variety of opportunities, at the right time of year, to attract breeding birds to your garden.

THE BREEDING CYCLE

The breeding behaviour of birds is amongst the most complex and fascinating in the whole of the animal kingdom. Scientists have studied it in great detail, yet there are still aspects of breeding behaviour that we do not fully understand.

After getting enough food to eat, breeding is the most important aspect of bird behaviour, because if a bird fails to reproduce, it cannot pass on its genes to a new generation of its species.

So by providing nesting sites for your garden's birds, you are not only helping them but giving yourself a grandstand view of the whole process – who needs Sir David Attenborough on the television when you've got a show like this going on outside your window?

Male birds sing for two reasons: to defend a territory against rival males and to attract and keep a mate. The Blackcap has an attractive, powerful song, full of fluty notes.

Males also defend their territories by displaying to intruding males. This Robin has adopted a threatening pose to put off a rival.

BIRDSONG AND TERRITORY

In early spring, as the days begin to lengthen, birds start to sing at full volume. If you're woken at 4 a.m. by the Song Thrush outside your window, console yourself with the fact that with songbird populations in decline, you are one of the lucky ones.

Male birds sing for two main reasons: to defend a territory against rival males and to attract a mate. The main times for singing are early in the morning – the 'dawn chorus' – and in the evening, although birds may sing at any time of the day, especially in spring. Birds often sing from a prominent place, such as on top of a roof or tree, where they can be seen and heard more easily by potential mates and rivals.

Some bird songs are simple, like the repetitive two-note call that gives the Cuckoo its name. Others are a complex outpouring of different notes and phrases, such as the celebrated songs of the Blackbird, the Song Thrush and the Robin.

COURTSHIP AND PAIR-FORMATION

When it comes to finding a mate, birds are notoriously lax in their moral standards – with polygamy and partner-swapping commonplace!

The Long-tailed Tit lines its nest with up to two thousand tiny feathers, which keep the eggs and chicks warm during cold weather in early spring.

In spring, watch out for territorial disputes between rival males. In the case of the Robin, these often take the form of vicious fights, which can result in injury to the vanquished bird, or even its death.

A more attractive aspect of spring behaviour is courtship display, in which several males may pay court to a single female. Courtship displays often appear quite amusing, as the male puffs himself up like a prizefighter, while the female turns away, apparently unimpressed.

Bear in mind, however, that you are watching a fundamental driving force of nature, with each bird trying to choose the healthiest mate in order to give its offspring the best chance of survival. This is evolution in the raw.

Once a pair has been formed, this is by no means the end of the story. Birds spend much of their time reinforcing the pair-bond by activities, such as mutual preening. Also, males must keep a wary eye out for other, unmated males, which may try to usurp their position.

BUILDING THE NEST

The next step in the breeding cycle is nest-building, usually undertaken by both partners. Nests come in all shapes and sizes, and may be made from natural or artificial materials.

One of the earliest garden birds to start nesting is the Blackbird, which often begins nest-building in March.

The nest is made from grasses woven together to form a cup, which is then lined with mud.

Many larger birds, such as Carrion Crows and Wood Pigeons, build their nests from sticks, often easily visible in the tops of a tree. Others, such as Jackdaws and Stock Doves, prefer to nest in holes, often taking over an old woodpecker hole where they can lay their eggs out of sight of predators.

Smaller birds will try to tuck their nests well out of sight, to avoid predators such as rats and mice, or egg-stealing birds such as Jays and Magpies. Some nests are little more than a tiny cup of moss and lichens, lined with a few feathers, such as the Goldcrest's; others are far more elaborate, such as the lichen-covered, ball-shaped nest of the Long-tailed Tit.

But all have one basic purpose: to keep the eggs safe and warm, and allow the adult birds to incubate their eggs and raise chicks.

EGGS: LAYING AND INCUBATION

A bird's egg is an extraordinary, almost miraculous object. Within its surprisingly sturdy shell the wonder of life begins: growing from a tiny embryo into a living, breathing chick, ready to take its place in the outside world and face the joys and hazards of life.

Blue Tits nest in tree-holes or artificial nestboxes, building a cup-shaped nest out of moss and grass, which they line with hair, wool and feathers. They lay up to sixteen eggs, though the usual number is around a dozen.

affects the supply of insect food.

The incubation period is often a quiet time, during which the female is sitting tight on the nest, while the male visits her from time to time to relieve her of her duties or to bring food.

HATCHING AND FEEDING YOUNG

Once the eggs have hatched, the busiest period in a bird's life begins. During every minute of daylight the parents are flying back and forth, attempting to provide enough food to satisfy their hungry chicks. This is a great opportunity to watch the birds really closely, as they are so concerned with feeding their young that they are not too bothered about anything else.

Most songbird chicks are born naked, blind and helpless, although they quickly grow a downy coat. After a few days, as their true feathers start to appear, they begin to look more and more like their parents.

FLEDGING AND LEAVING THE NEST

The period before the young fledge (gain their flight feathers and leave the nest) also varies tremendously from species to species. The young of some birds, such as Blackcaps, fledge after as little as eight days, but most songbird young fledge after about two weeks. Young of larger species, such as pigeons, take longer to fledge: around three to five weeks, by which time they may be outgrowing their rickety nest.

A hungry brood of Blue Tit chicks wait expectantly for their parent to return with food – usually a succulent caterpillar or two.

Once the nest is ready, the female will begin to lay her eggs: usually one a day laid in the early morning, until the clutch is complete. Only then will she start to incubate, a process that ensures that all the eggs hatch more or less at the same time.

Clutch sizes vary tremendously, from a single egg, in the case of many seabirds, to two dozen or more, for gamebirds such as the Pheasant. Typical garden birds lay anything from three to five eggs (House Martin, Mistle Thrush), to as many as a dozen (Blue Tit).

Incubation periods can also vary, from as short as eleven days for some Pied Wagtails, to as long as four weeks, in the case of Swifts. The Swift varies its incubation period depending on the weather, which

This young Blue Tit is only about three weeks old, yet it is now about to fledge and will soon leave the nest to face the dangers of the outside world.

SECOND BROODS

And third, and fourth, and even fifth broods! Not all birds are satisfied with raising a single brood of young in the same season. Almost as soon as the young from the first brood have fledged, many species will embark on the process all over again.

Some will go on as long as time, weather and the food supply allow. House Sparrows often raise three or four broods and Blackbirds sometimes manage five. The female Blackbird may even begin laying a new clutch while her partner is feeding the young from the previous brood. Nevertheless, some garden birds, including most species of tits and crows, follow a rather different strategy: raising just one brood of young. They compensate by investing greater care, aiming to raise a higher proportion of chicks to adulthood.

Many migrants, such as Spotted Flycatcher and Turtle Dove, vary the numbers of broods they raise from season to season, depending on weather conditions. Because they have only a limited time to breed before returning south, they need dry and warm weather during the summer months if they are to succeed in rearing a second brood.

THE QUIET PERIOD

During the month of July, everything in the garden suddenly goes quiet. Where before there was birdsong and a flurry of breeding activity, now there is only silence. There are two reasons for this: first, the male birds have stopped singing because there is no longer any need to defend a territory or attract a mate; and second, the adults are undergoing their annual moult. This term describes the process of shedding old, worn feathers, and their replacement by new, fresh ones. If birds did not moult, their plumage would soon become so bedraggled and damaged that their ability to fly would be affected.

THREATS TO NESTING BIRDS

Nesting birds are vulnerable to all sorts of threats. Wind may blow down the nest, heavy rain prevent the eggs from hatching, or newborn young may die of exposure. Early in the year, an unseasonal frost or snowfall may prevent the adults from finding food, leaving the chicks to starve.

Predators are another major threat. Domestic cats, squirrels, rodents, Jays and Magpies are all on the lookout for a tasty and nutritious snack at this time of year. If one of the adults falls victim to a predator, the chicks usually die of starvation. However, if a clutch is lost for whatever reason, most birds will make another attempt to nest.

Finally, human beings! Despite having their best interests at heart, we can pose a danger to nesting birds, simply by disturbing them. It can be very tempting to keep looking at a nest, especially when there are eggs or chicks. But beware! You may prevent the parents from bringing food back for hungry chicks, or cause an incubating bird to fly away, exposing the nest to danger. Also, make sure you avoid damaging foliage which may be shielding the nest from the attention of predators. If you do need to inspect the nest, keep your visit as brief as possible, and avoid doing so in cold or wet weather.

Although essentially a shy bird, the Jay will occasionally rob small birds' nests when it is rearing young. A properly constructed nest box should avoid this problem.

However, the period when birds are moulting can be a dangerous time for them, as the loss of feathers makes them vulnerable to predators. Moulting in mid-summer reduces the danger, because at that time there are lots of places to shelter, plentiful supplies of food, and the weather is warm enough to allow them to bear the effects of the temporary loss of plumage.

Moult can take as little as a month for many migrants, which must grow a fresh plumage before they undertake their long journey south, to almost three months for some resident species.

Care of Young Birds

Which brings me to the thorny subject of what you should do when you find a baby bird which appears to have fallen out of the nest.

Last year the RSPB received more than ten thousand telephone enquiries on this subject. Many callers were worried that the young bird would fall victim to the local cat, or that it had lost its parents and would starve to death. Many felt that they ought to do something.

However, all may not be quite as it seems. When young birds first leave the nest they often appear helpless, and indeed are usually still under the care of one or both parents. The adults may be away finding food, or may have been frightened off by your presence.

Some young birds look nothing like their parents. This juvenile Robin lacks the adults' orange breast, and is streaked and spotted instead.

In response to these enquiries, the RSPB has produced a useful 'code of conduct', with a helpful set of guidelines on what to do in such circumstances:

- it is most important to resist the temptation to bring the bird indoors immediately;
- if it appears to be unfeathered, it has probably fallen out of the nest. You can try to find the nest and put it back, although this can be tricky, and it is probably better to humanely destroy the chick;
- if it has feathers, but is not yet able to fly, it has almost certainly left the nest voluntarily or at the urgings of its parents. They will soon return to the nest, provided that you are not disturbing them;
- if the bird is in an exposed position, perhaps on an open lawn, it may be a good idea to place it in some cover: by the edge of a flower-bed or a shrubbery, where the parents will be able to find it without difficulty;

As birds moult out of their juvenile plumage they begin to look more like their parents. The spotting on this young Starling is a sign of adult plumage.

Above: *Nestboxes can be designed for any species which regularly nests in a hole: even one as large as this Tawny Owl.*

Left: *Some nestboxes blend in better with their environment than others. This Blue Tit is bringing back a caterpillar to its young, to a nestbox made from an old log with a twig for a perch.*

● once you have done this, go away for an hour or two. In most cases the parents will have returned, fed the chick, and everything will be all right;

● if, when you return, the bird is still there, you can take it home, but this really should be as a last resort. It is not easy to act as a substitute parent, and the chances are the fledgling will soon die.

If you are still unsure what action to take, ring your local RSPCA (the number will be listed in your local telephone directory). Alternatively, you can contact the RSPB Enquiry Unit on 01767 680551. The Unit is open from Mondays to Fridays, from 9 a.m. to 5.15 p.m., and is staffed with experts who will be able to help you.

Finally, bear in mind that all birds have far greater numbers of young than they can possibly raise to adulthood. Most are killed by predators, or die of disease or natural causes before they are one year old.

NESTBOXES

After giving food and water, the next best thing you can do to attract birds to your garden is to provide one or more nestboxes.

Nestboxes are simply manufactured substitutes for natural nest sites. With a serious shortage of natural holes in trees suitable for species such as tits, nestboxes are a vitally important way of helping our garden birds. Always buy a nestbox from a reputable supplier, such as the RSPB (*see* Useful Addresses page 157), as it will be designed with the birds' welfare in mind.

Nestbox Designs

Nestboxes come in all sorts of shapes and sizes, each designed to attract a particular species, or group of species. The most popular nestbox design consists of a rectangular box with a small hole in the front, about

Above: *Once the eggs have hatched, baby chicks need plenty of food. Both male and female Pied Flycatchers spend most of the time gathering insect food for their hungry young.*

Above right: *A large, sturdy, open-fronted nestbox is an ideal home for this family of young Kestrels.*

three-quarters of the way up. Depending on the diameter of the hole, this will attract Blue or Great Tits, but may also be suitable for House or Tree Sparrows.

The other basic design is open-fronted, to attract species such as Robin, Spotted Flycatcher or Pied Wagtail.

A nestbox is usually made of wood, but recent versions on the market include one made from a mixture of concrete and sawdust, known as 'woodcrete'. The makers claim the woodcrete box has a longer life and is better for the birds because it reduces condensation and humidity, and also keeps the eggs and chicks at a more constant temperature. However, 'woodcrete' nestboxes are slightly more expensive than standard wooden models.

SPECIALIZED NESTBOXES

If you really get bitten by the nestbox bug, you can buy or make a box designed to attract most garden species, even those as big as Kestrel or Tawny Owl. The many specialized nestboxes include those designed for

Treecreepers, which resemble a cavity in the bark of a tree; and for House Martins, which can be placed underneath the eaves of your roof, preferably facing north or east. One or two artificial House Martin nests sometimes have the effect of attracting other birds to build their nests nearby, and so create a new colony.

BUYING A NESTBOX

If you buy your nestbox from a reputable supplier, such as the RSPB *(see Useful Addresses page 157)*, not only will it be the best design for the birds' needs, and most likely to attract them, but it will also be built to last and will come with a guarantee.

Prices start at around £10, although you may have to pay £30 or more for specialized boxes.

Above: *Hole-nesting species such as tits readily adapt to artificial nestboxes. The Great Tit prefers a slightly larger entrance hole than its smaller relative, the Blue Tit.*

How to Make a Nestbox

If these prices make you or your bank manager shudder, why not have a go at making your own nestbox? You don't have to be a DIY fanatic – after all, the basic model consists simply of six pieces of wood and a hole.

The first thing you need to know about making your own nestbox is that it does not have to follow a perfect design, or even be a standard size. After all, natural nest sites do not come in regular shapes and sizes, yet the birds still use them.

The basic tools and equipment you will need to construct a nestbox are:
• a **plank of wood**, roughly 1–1.5 m (39–58 in) long, and 150 mm (6 in) wide and about 15–20 mm (0.6–0.8 in) thick.
• a sharp **wood saw.**
• **galvanized nails**, **panel pins** or **wood screws.**
• a **strip of leather**, **rubber** or **heavy-duty carpet tape** to hinge the lid and a hook and eye to make it secure.
• a **manual** or **power drill**, with a suitably sized cutting blade for making the entrance hole.
• a **tape measure**.

TO ASSEMBLE THE NESTBOX:

1. First, mark out your plank with the dimensions of the box, given in the diagram on the right. Note that the back panel can vary in size depending on where you wish to fix the box, but it should have a minimum length of 250 mm (10 in).

2. Cut the wood into six pieces, being particularly careful to keep cuts straight and at right angles to the edge of the plank. The exception to this is the cut between the two side pieces, which should be made at a shallow angle.

3. Drill two small holes at the top and bottom of the back panel, for fixing the completed box.

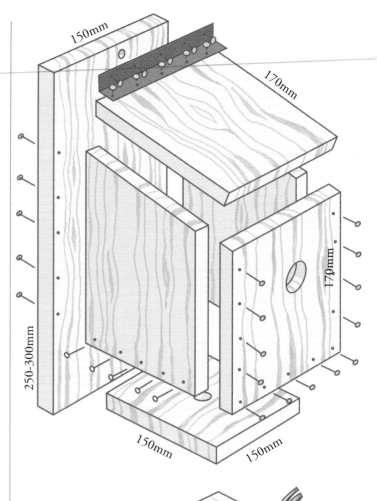

4. Nail or screw the two side panels to the base, approximately equidistant from each end.

5. Drill a hole in the front panel, approximately 125 mm (5 in) from the bottom. The hole can vary in size from 25 mm (1 in) for smaller tits such as Blue and Coal Tit; to 28 mm (1.1 in) for Great Tits; and 32 mm (1.25 in) for House Sparrows, Tree Sparrows and Nuthatches.

6. Drill a small hole in the base to allow water to drain out of the nestbox.

7. Nail or screw the base and front panel to the box.

8. Fix the roof, using a strip of leather, rubber, or heavy duty sticky carpet tape to make a hinge. Make sure there is a short overhang to keep out the rain. Make the lid secure, either using a couple of panel pins, or if you want to be able to inspect the contents, with a hook and eye.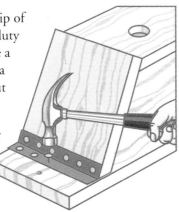

9. Before you put your box up, treat the exterior with a wood-preserving agent such as creosote or one of the branded preservers such as Cuprinol or Fenceguard. Never treat the inside of the box, as this may cause harm to the birds.

10. If you have squirrels or woodpeckers in your garden, fix a metal plate around the hole to prevent forced entry.

Siting a Nestbox

Once you've bought or made your nestbox, you now have to decide where to put it. It's worth following a few basic rules:

● put your box up in autumn or winter, so that the birds have a chance to notice it and get used to it before the breeding season begins;
● fix your box on a tree, wall or garden fence, 1.6–5 m (5–16 ft) above ground level. Use sturdy nails or screws if attaching to a post or fence, or hang from a wire if attaching to a tree;
● site the box facing in any direction between north and south-east to avoid strong sunlight, prevailing winds and rain. Try to tilt the front of the box downwards a little, to create an overhang that will keep out rain;
● site the box out of reach of cats, and away from perches that could be used by bird predators or reached by squirrels. Also keep the box away from a bird table or feeders, as the presence of feeding birds nearby will put off potential occupants;
● if you are putting up more than one nestbox, avoid siting them too close together, as this may lead to aggression between rival males;
● when siting a nestbox, always be concerned for your own safety. Be especially careful when using tools, and when climbing a ladder to site your nestbox;

Be careful when siting your nestbox: this box is placed far too low on the tree, making it difficult for the birds to enter and presenting an easy target for predators such as squirrels and cats.

● be patient. Garden birds may take a little while to get used to a nestbox, and you may have to wait as long as a whole year before it is occupied;
● once the birds have taken up residence, resist the temptation to inspect the nestbox too often. The BTO have produced a code of conduct for nest inspection, for the use of people participating in their Nest Record Scheme *(see page 63)*;
● every autumn, after you are sure all the young have fledged, clean the box thoroughly, removing any loose debris and scrubbing it inside. Avoid strong chemical cleaners, however. Use boiling water to kill parasites, or lightly dust the interior of the box with a natural insecticide such as pyrethrum powder.

This nestbox is also in the wrong place: facing south, where it receives the full glare of the midday sun. In hot weather, the chicks will soon overheat and die.

The best place to put a nestbox is several metres up a tree or fence post, facing away from the glare of the midday sun.

● on inspecting your box after the end of the breeding season, you may discover unhatched eggs or dead young. Don't worry about these, as it is normal for some nesting attempts to end in failure. You may legally remove and dispose of unhatched eggs between October and January.

If you want to find out more about nestboxes, the BTO have produced an excellent practical guide. 'Nestboxes', by Chris du Feu, is available by mail order direct from the BTO, price £5.95, including postage and packing (*see* Useful Addresses page 157 for details).

OTHER NEST SITES AND MATERIALS

Birds are highly adaptable, and many species have learned to take advantage of the presence of human beings. Robins are a fine example: every year there are reports of a Robin nesting somewhere unusual, such as in a hanging basket, watering can or even on top of a lavatory cistern! Spotted Flycatchers, will also nest anywhere suitable they can find. Surprisingly, perhaps, nesting in peculiar places does not appear to affect the birds' eventual breeding success.

You can help birds by providing nesting material, too. Many species use animal hair or feathers to line their nests, so put out suitable material during the early part of the breeding season.

One manufacturer has come up with a clever solution to a problem faced by House Martins. Summer droughts have reduced the supply of mud suitable for making their nests, sometimes leading to breeding failure. So now you can buy 'House Martin mud', which you put out on a tray for the birds to collect. In an ingenious twist, the mud is coloured blue, so you can measure its success by seeing how blue your local nests are!

Birds will nest in all sorts of odd places! This Spotted Flycatcher has chosen to raise its young inside an old hand mincer!

The BTO also organizes National Nestbox Week, an event which takes place from February 14th each year, and aims to encourage people to provide nestboxes for their garden birds. For further details, contact the BTO.

THE BTO NEST RECORD SCHEME

Started back in 1939, at the start of the Second World War, the BTO's Nest Record Scheme is the oldest project of its type in the world. Its aim is to record the breeding success or failure of Britain's breeding species.

You can participate in the scheme by getting in touch with the BTO (see Useful Addresses page 157). They will send you record cards and details of how to fill them in. The scheme is particularly good at giving us early warning of rises and declines in bird populations.

In 1995, the Scheme passed a notable landmark: the one millionth card was submitted – a Pied Wagtail nesting in the outbuilding of a croft located in the Highlands of Scotland.

White Storks tend to breed in nests made of big sticks on the roofs of houses, but are only occasional summer visitors to the British Isles.

While Wrens are happy to nest in open-fronted nest boxes – and even tit boxes - this tiny species will also make a concealed nest in a suitable gap in a stone wall.

The largest European thrush, the Mistle Thrush builds a grass-lined nest, often – as here- in the fork of a tree.

5

PESTS,
PREDATORS &
OTHER HAZARDS

*"The Creator must have had an inordinate
fondness for beetles"*.

J.B.S. HALDANE

GARDEN WARS

*When you begin to attract birds to your garden, it may not be long before you come up
against a problem. A squirrel may rob your bird table or damage your peanut feeder; a
cat might drop your beloved Robin at your feet; or perhaps a bird will fly into your plate
glass window and stun itself.*

There are many hazards involved in encouraging birds to visit your garden. As you deal with rats, mice, Jays, Magpies, Sparrowhawks, Herons, foxes, and a whole host of invertebrate pests, you may sometimes think that your garden is the battleground in a particularly violent war.

So what can you do to stop, or at least restrain, the marauding hordes? Total warfare is time-consuming and likely to be counter-productive. Instead, you must be willing to enter into diplomatic compromise, being firm but fair. Aim for a degree of tolerance, not mutually assured destruction!

INSECTS AND INVERTEBRATE PESTS

The very word 'pest' is an emotive one. Insects may damage plants, but they are also a valuable source of food for our garden birds. So how do you strike a balance between preserving the beauty of your garden, and providing natural food for the birds?

For most gardeners, the most notorious pests are caterpillars, snails, slugs and aphids, because of the very visible damage they cause to the leaves of flowering plants.

There are several different ways of dealing with these, some more effective than others. Whichever method you choose is up to you, but be aware of the consequences of using the more radical solutions such as pesticides.

NATURAL PEST CONTROL METHODS

You can reduce, though not entirely eliminate, the damage caused by these pests by employing some simple but effective methods, which will not cause any harm to the environment:

*One of the most common garden pests is the introduced Grey
Squirrel, which has become highly skilled at pilfering food
from peanut feeders.*

Aphids, or greenfly, are harmful parasites, loathed by gardeners everywhere. Rather than use chemical warfare, why not try encouraging the aphids' natural predators, such as ladybirds?

• keep your garden tidy: remove pots and containers and sweep up autumn leaves to take away hiding-places for slugs and snails;

• keep the garden healthy: well-watered and well-fed plants resist predation;

• encourage hedgehogs and other animal predators to reduce slug numbers rapidly. Amphibians such as frogs and toads mainly feed on insects and slugs;

• encourage a wide variety of bird predators. The best way to keep down the amount of pests in your garden is to have a thriving population of Song Thrushes, which prey on snails, and Blue and Great Tits, which eat caterpillars;

• encourage 'good' insect predators, such as ladybirds, which will keep the aphid population in check;

• use organic or biological treatments recommended by the Henry Doubleday Research Association *(see* Useful Addresses page 157). These include environmentally friendly types of slug powder, and treatments that use one living organism to control another, such as a predatory midge that kills aphids.

PESTICIDES

In the climate of optimism during the years following World War II, pesticides were hailed as a miracle cure for our farmers and gardeners. Chemicals like DDT, it was claimed, would remove the harmful insect pests and allow crops and plants to flourish.

With hindsight, we can see that this was a very naïve belief indeed. The population crash of birds of prey such as the Sparrowhawk and Peregrine, during the 1950s and early 1960s, was mainly due to the long-term, cumulative effects of these so-called miracle pesticides. These became concentrated as they rose up the food chain, and were eventually discovered to cause a thinning of eggshells, which resulted in a catastrophic drop in breeding success.

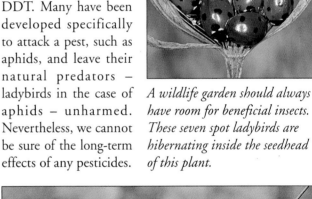

Garden pesticides produced today are believed to be nowhere near as harmful as DDT. Many have been developed specifically to attack a pest, such as aphids, and leave their natural predators – ladybirds in the case of aphids – unharmed. Nevertheless, we cannot be sure of the long-term effects of any pesticides.

A wildlife garden should always have room for beneficial insects. These seven spot ladybirds are hibernating inside the seedhead of this plant.

Slugs and snails cause a lot of damage to garden plants, but they also provide a valuable source of food for birds such as the Song Thrush.

The Long-tailed Tit amply demonstrates natural predation of undesirable insects such as caterpillars, which can cause havoc amongst leafy plants.

My advice is to limit the use of pesticides in the garden as far as is possible and to use organic methods of control whenever this is feasible.

The use of pesticides can easily lead you into a vicious circle from which it is hard to escape. Some pesticides continue to kill 'good' creatures as well as 'bad' ones, thus removing the main natural predators from a garden. Also, by reducing the total amount of invertebrate life, on which birds feed, you will eventually reduce the bird population in your garden.

Above: Although it frequently takes songbirds from gardens, the Sparrowhawk at least has the virtue of being a natural predator, unlike the domestic cat.

LARGER ANIMAL PESTS AND PREDATORS

Despite the small size and urban or suburban location of many gardens, it's amazing just how many animals manage to survive there. The urban fox has become justly famous, carrying out nocturnal raids on dustbins with a practised nonchalance. The introduced American Grey Squirrel is equally well-known; rats and mice live largely unseen in and around our homes and gardens.

FOXES

Foxes should not be a major problem in most gardens, but nevertheless it is worth taking a few precautions against them. Always keep your rubbish bags in a dustbin with a tight-fitting lid, rather than leave them out where the foxes will discover them. And remember to clean up any uneaten food remaining on or underneath the bird table each evening.

SQUIRRELS

Of all the mammals found in the garden, it is perhaps the squirrel which has become the greatest pest. Squirrels have developed a liking for peanuts, and their acrobatic skills and strong jaws mean that few bird feeders are immune from a squirrel's attempts to gnaw through the outer casing to get at their contents.

For many years, the manufacturers of bird feeders were engaged in a constant war against the squirrel, developing ever more ingenious products that claim to be

Right: Grey Squirrels are skilled acrobats, able to make short work of a plastic bird feeder in order to get at the peanuts inside.

squirrel-proof, then watching helplessly as the ingenious squirrel managed to effect an entry. Today, they seem finally to have gained the upper hand, with a wide range of squirrel-resistant nut and seed feeders. Most follow the same basic design, in which the feeder part of the device is enclosed in a strong wire cage, thus letting the smaller birds in but keeping squirrels (and larger birds, such as Starlings) out.

To prevent squirrels climbing up a pole onto a bird table, the simplest solution is to cut a length of plastic drainpipe, place it around the pole a few centimetres from the top, then cut a hole in a biscuit tin, and place it on top of the pipe, beneath the base of the table. This will prevent squirrels from reaching the food.

During the breeding season, squirrels present a hazard to nesting birds, as they will readily take eggs and young chicks from the nest. Unfortunately, short of guarding each nest, there is not very much you can do to prevent nests from being robbed by squirrels.

RATS AND MICE

Rats and mice are attracted to surplus food, so you should follow a few simple rules to discourage them:

- never put out too much food at once, especially on a bird table;
- always clean up around a bird table each evening, paying special attention to any spilt food on the ground;
- always store bird food in a secure place, and in strong, sealed containers.

BEWARE OF THE CAT!

All these 'natural' pests and predators, even the introduced grey squirrel, pale into insignificance when it comes to *Felis catus*, the domestic cat. As a killer of our garden birds, it is in a league of its own; and because it is a domestic or feral animal, it has no natural predators to keep it in check. On the other hand, many bird-lovers are cat-lovers too, so we must try to find a solution to the problem which will keep both sides happy.

CATS: THE FACTS AND FIGURES

Our domestic cats are descended from the African wildcat, *Felis libyca*, and were probably spread throughout the world by sailors, who used them to catch rats and mice on board ship.

According to the RSPCA, there are approximately 7.2 million cats living in the United Kingdom, of which between 2 and 3 million, or about one in three, are living in a feral state.

They are natural and highly effective predators, and in the enclosed setting of a typical garden they find the ideal combination of availability and opportunity: a feeding-station to attract the birds, and plenty of bushes and trees where they can hide before pouncing.

The numbers of birds killed by cats each year is unknown, although one recent estimate suggests that the number of casualties may be as high as 75 million birds every year. This is the equivalent of the entire breeding population of our top ten most common birds.

However, this figure has not gone unchallenged, and one reputable biologist has claimed that the figure could be as low as 28 million. This is still very high, but not quite so horrific as the first estimate.

If you have a cat, try putting a bell onto its collar. The noise made by the bell will act as a warning signal to birds that a predator is on the loose.

CATS: THE CASE AGAINST

The controversy over cat predation doesn't stop there. There are a number of arguments why cats are more harmful to birds than 'natural' predators such as Sparrowhawks or Magpies:

● cats are introduced predators, which means there is no natural check on their numbers;
● domestic cats are fed and housed, thus prolonging their life and allowing them to kill more birds;
● cats mainly kill adult birds, therefore have a greater effect on long-term bird populations than other predators, which mainly take eggs or chicks;
● cats kill their prey slowly, causing greater suffering than other predators.

CATS: THE CASE FOR

Proponents of cats accept that they do some harm, but argue that they have little long-term effect on bird populations, for the following reasons:

If you want to keep a cat without harming the birds, why not get a white one? Studies have shown that white cats are the least effective predators of all.

● the numbers of birds killed by cats may have been grossly overestimated (*see* page 69);
● cats kill individual birds, but there is little or no evidence to suggest that bird populations are affected in the longer term;
● cats also kill other animals, such as rats and mice, that are harmful to birds;
● most feral cats in towns and cities rarely catch prey, and survive by scavenging and on waste food;
● cats are much-loved and valuable companions to humans, particularly older people or those living alone.

CATS: WHAT CAN YOU DO?

Whichever of the two arguments you believe, there is no doubt that cats do cause a degree of suffering to garden birds. Furthermore, it can be unpleasant to have to clear up every time your cat brings in a mangled corpse. So why not try some measures designed to control cats and reduce their chances of killing your garden birds?

● position your bird table, bird feeders and nestboxes out of reach of cats. If you are unsure where to put them, experiment with a couple of different positions first, and watch out to see how well the cats are discouraged;
● if you own a cat, put a large, loud bell around its neck, which should act as a warning to the birds;
● have your cat neutered so that you don't add to the feral cat population – especially if you own a tomcat;
● during the breeding season, especially when chicks begin to fledge and leave the nest, keep your cat well fed and indoors as much as possible.

Research also indicates that some breeds of cat are far more successful at hunting than others. Siamese cats are the champion killers, described by one observer as "the Rambo of the cat world", closely followed by black cats. The most bird-friendly cats were white ones, which failed to catch any birds. So if you want to provide a home for a cat, and protect birds, choose a white cat.

BIRD PREDATORS

Some garden birds fall into two categories: to some people they are a welcome visitor, to others, a lethal predator. The best-known predators are probably the Jay and the Magpie, whose recent population increases have led to campaigns for their reduction.

Among other predators are the Sparrowhawk, whose numbers are also increasing, the Grey Heron, the

Left: *The Magpie is an opportunistic predator, frequently taking eggs or chicks from nests. However, there is no evidence that this reduces the population of our common songbirds.*

Below: *Kestrels sometimes feed on small birds, although they are fairly unusual visitors to gardens, preferring to hunt over more open ground.*

Kingfisher, and even the Great Spotted Woodpecker, which regularly preys on the eggs and chicks of smaller birds.

The aim must be to strike a balance. These are all natural predators which need to eat to survive, and none of them has been proved to have a significant effect on long-term bird populations. However, in an artificial garden environment you may unwittingly create a situation where the predator gains the upper hand. So you should sometimes take steps to redress the balance in favour of the prey.

THE MAGPIE CONTROVERSY

The Magpie population has increased dramatically in recent years, while some of our familiar garden birds, such as the Song Thrush and House Sparrow, have been decreasing in numbers. Many people have, quite understandably, made a connection between the two events, and blame Magpies for the songbirds' decline.

The truth about Magpies is less dramatic, but far more reassuring. Yes, Magpies, like their cousin the Jay, do take the eggs and chicks of other birds. Yes, this may result in fewer birds breeding in your garden, especially if there is a thriving Magpie population in your area.

However, scientists have proved that it is the population of the predator that rises or falls depending on the availability of prey, not the other way around. In effect, this means that Magpies are taking the surplus of each season's eggs and chicks. The result is that Magpie predation has little or no long-term effect on the population of songbird species.

In fact, we are seeing the results of two very different events. In the past, Magpies had one main enemy: gamekeepers, who would shoot every Magpie they saw. In recent years, a decline in the persecution of Magpies by gamekeepers has allowed the population to thrive and increase; while the spread of modern farming methods, with a resulting shortage of food available for birds, has caused our songbird populations to fall. The two events appear to be connected, but this is simply coincidence.

Nevertheless, there are steps you can take to protect nesting birds against predation by Magpies and Jays:
● plant bushes and shrubs which provide plenty of dense vegetation in which small birds can nest out of sight;
● if you find a nest, place small gauge mesh wire netting around the entrance. This lets the adults in, while keeping larger predators out;

The Sparrowhawk will pounce on small birds, using its sharp talons to kill them and to keep hold of its prey while feeding. This bird has recently finished a tasty meal.

● place mesh wire netting around the entrance to your nestboxes. This is best carried out while the eggs are being incubated rather than during nest-building, as if done at this early stage birds may desert the nest.

SPARROWHAWKS

There can be few more dramatic sights in an ordinary garden than that of a Sparrowhawk shooting through the trees to snatch an unsuspecting Blue Tit off a bird table, before plucking it on a nearby post.

Many people find such a sight a thrilling example of nature in action; others are upset by witnessing the killing. But it is important to remember that Sparrowhawks are natural predators, and that they always kill their prey quickly.

Moreover, scientists have shown that although Sparrowhawk populations have increased substantially in the last two decades, thanks to the banning of agricultural chemicals such as DDT, they have no significant effect on songbird populations.

Sparrowhawks are not immune to danger themselves. Because they fly so fast and low, they frequently fall victim to hazards such as plate glass windows (*see* page 73); and in one extraordinary case a hunting Sparrowhawk was itself attacked and killed by a Magpie!

Finally, bear in mind that without the presence of Sparrowhawks we would soon be, as one ornithologist memorably described it, "knee-deep in Great Tits".

OTHER BIRD PREDATORS

Many other species of bird will occasionally prey on smaller species. For example, Great Spotted Woodpeckers frequently hack their way into nestboxes in search of eggs or chicks for food. The obvious solution is to place a metal plate around the hole to deter them.

Two of the most welcome predators to a garden must be the Grey Heron and the Kingfisher. Loss of fish from a garden pond is more than made up for by the spectacle of these magnificent hunters. Nevertheless, it can be frustrating to lose all your goldfish, or even a native population of frogs or newts, to a marauding heron.

DETERRING HERONS

Fortunately, there are several steps you can take to reduce the number of fish taken:

1. **Scaring**: using visual devices such as scarecrows, streamers or flashing lights, or audio devices such as electronic noise-makers or gas cannons. However, these remedies may not remain effective for very long, because herons have been known to get used to them (*see* Useful Addresses page 157, for further details).
2. **Model herons**: in theory, the presence of a model heron should deter a visiting wild bird, as herons defend feeding territories in summer and winter. However, it is also possible that such a device may attract the attention of a passing heron.
3. **Animals** and **children**: dogs, or the noise of children playing, may be effective in scaring a heron away. However, because herons usually feed in the early morning or late evening, these may not prove a very practical deterrent.
4. **Pond design**: steep banks make it difficult for the heron to feed, and plenty of floating vegetation in the pond itself, or surrounding the pond with bushes and trees, may also put them off.
5. **Added extras**: spray from a fountain deters herons by making it hard for them to see their prey. Running a criss-cross network of strings, net or wire across the pond surface also makes feeding more difficult. Make sure you keep the netting taut, and choose a small enough mesh size (10–15 cm or 4–6in), so that the heron cannot reach through the netting to the fish below.

OTHER GARDEN HAZARDS

There are a number of other hazards lurking in your garden, which may not be obvious at first, but which if left unattended will sooner or later cause injury or death to your garden birds.

GLASS WINDOWS AND DOORS

Each year many thousands of birds are killed in our gardens because of collisions with plate glass windows or doors. This usually happens either because they are confused by seeing their reflection in the glass, or because they catch sight of another window beyond the first and think they can fly straight through.

Almost any species can fall victim to this hazard, although low-flying predators such as the Sparrowhawk are particularly vulnerable.

Birds may also attack their own reflection in a window, mistaking it for a rival male entering their territory. This is less important, as it is unlikely to result in serious injury.

The best solution to the problem of collisions is to fix some kind of object to the inside of the door or window, which lets the bird know that the glass is solid. Almost any shape will do, although some people prefer to use a silhouette of a hawk, which they believe has an extra deterrent effect. You can make this yourself out of coloured self-adhesive plastic, or buy a ready-made one. Alternatively, why not use a specially designed bird feeder with suction pads to attach to the glass?

WATER TUBS AND BARRELS

Tubs to collect rainwater are an attractive asset to any garden, but can be lethal to birds, especially during hot, dry weather, when other sources of water dry up. A bird attempting to drink or bathe can easily slip, and because of the steep sides it is unable to escape from the tub. Without help, its plumage will soon become waterlogged, and it will drown. You can avoid this by placing a plank across the top of the water, which will allow the bird to drink without falling into the tub.

BIRDS AND THE LAW

It is well worth making yourself familiar with some of the specific areas of the law that relate to garden birds.

Birds, their nests and eggs are protected under the Wildlife and Countryside Act 1981 against a number of threats. It is illegal to do any of the following:

Kingfishers may take fish from your garden pond – but this seems a small price to pay to observe this beautiful bird at close quarters.

- kill or injure any wild bird;
- trap, capture or take into captivity any wild bird;
- take or destroy the egg of any wild bird.

However, there are a few exceptions. So-called 'pest species' including crows, Woodpigeon, House Sparrow and Starling can be killed, or their eggs destroyed, by authorized people (including farmers). Gamebirds such as Pheasant and Partridge may also be shot during the appropriate season.

Also, you may take an injured wild bird into captivity, so long as you intend to release it when it recovers. If it is beyond recovery, you may kill it humanely.

If you see anyone killing, attempting to kill, or trapping wild birds, by whatever means, or you suspect that someone is collecting eggs in your area, your first step should be to contact your local police station immediately, and ask for the Wildlife Liaison Officer. If this does not produce a satisfactory result, contact the RSPB direct, asking for the Enquiry Unit *(see* Useful Addresses page 157, for further details). By taking prompt action, you may save birds' lives.

6

DIRECTORY OF GARDEN BIRDS

GREY HERON

Ardea cinerea Length 90–100 cm (36–40 in)

If you have a pond in your garden, sooner or later it is bound to attract a visiting heron. Depending on how much you value your fish, this may or may not be a welcome sight! With its huge neck, broad wings and dagger-like beak, the heron is by far the largest garden bird in the British Isles. Herons usually visit gardens early in the morning, as they are shy birds, and will usually flee at the sight of humans.

IDENTIFICATION

If you get a good view of this bird, it is impossible to mistake it. Upright posture. Plumage mainly grey; white neck and breast spotted with black; white head with black stripe extending from eye to back of neck. Beak and legs yellow. Juvenile generally duller, with less well-marked head pattern. In flight, very broad wings, hunched neck and long, trailing legs. Call a deep, far-carrying 'fraaannk'.

IN THE GARDEN

STATUS AND HABITAT: A frequent visitor to gardens with ponds, or those near water. May also be seen in flight overhead, its huge silhouette and slow, deliberate flight distinguishing it from crows and large gulls.

BREEDING: Breeds in large, communal colonies ('heronries'), away from gardens.

FEEDING: Feeds mainly on fish and frogs, though in harsh winter weather may be forced to take a more catholic diet, including rodents and small birds.

Above: *Grey Herons are highly efficient hunters, feeding mainly on fish and frogs. They may be observed stalking their prey, before attacking with a sudden lunge of their huge, powerful bill.*

Left: *Grey Herons typically breed in large colonies, known as 'heronries', building their huge nests out of twigs. The breeding season starts early, often before there are leaves on the trees.*

WHITE STORK

Ciconia ciconia Length 100–115 cm (40–45 in)

One of Europe's best-known birds, the White Stork is a familiar sight in many towns and villages, where it is believed to bring good luck. However, it remains a very rare visitor to the British Isles, usually appearing in fine weather during spring. In recent years Europe's stork population has declined, disappearing completely from many parts of the continent.

IDENTIFICATION

With its huge size, dagger-shaped bill and black-and-white plumage, the White Stork is unmistakable, whether in flight or at rest. Storks perch in an upright stance, giving them an almost human appearance at times. Head, neck, breast and back are white, with the lower part of the wings a contrasting black colour. Huge, orange-red beak, and long legs, also orange-red. In flight, shows white plumage and broad, black wings. Migrates in huge flocks, often soaring high in the sky. Often clatters its bill, making an extraordinary sound.

A pair of White Storks mating. They build their huge nest out of sticks, usually on a rooftop. Pairs of White Storks return from Africa in April, always remaining faithful to their place of birth.

IN THE GARDEN

STATUS AND HABITAT: Storks are familiar summer visitors to towns and villages in various parts of Europe, including Spain, France, Germany, Denmark and eastern Europe. However, due to climatic change, modern farming methods and pollution, the White Stork has recently declined over most of its range.

BREEDING: Breeds from April to July, building a huge nest from sticks, on the roof of a large house or church, or on a man-made platform. Lays 4 white eggs, and incubates for 4–5 weeks. Young fledge after 8–9 weeks. One brood.

FEEDING: Feeds on a wide variety of prey, including rodents, amphibians and large insects, usually taken from the ground.

The White Stork is a familiar bird of towns and villages across rural Europe, where it is believed to bring good luck to the local community. Storks feed mainly on rodents, frogs and large insects.

MALLARD

Anas platyrhynchos Length 51–62 cm (20–24 in)

The commonest and best-known 'wild duck' in north-west Europe, although many are actually descended from captive birds, bred and released for sport. Mallards are usually found in freshwater habitats such as lakes, but may pay a visit to the smallest garden pond, or graze on a damp lawn. On larger ponds they sometimes stay to feed, and if left undisturbed will occasionally even nest in gardens.

IDENTIFICATION

Male handsome and distinctive, with bottle-green head, yellow bill and deep magenta breast. Rest of plumage greyish-buff, with black under tail. Female mottled brown, with darker crown, dark stripe through eye, pale yellow bill and purple 'speculum' (patch on wing). Beware males in 'eclipse' plumage during summer months, when bright colours fade owing to moult.

IN THE GARDEN

STATUS AND HABITAT: Found occasionally in gardens with ponds, or those near suitable areas of fresh water.
BREEDING: Breeds from February to August, nesting in a wide variety of sites, including on the ground or in holes in trees. Lays 9–12 large, greenish-buff or cream-coloured eggs, and incubates for 4 weeks. Young leave nest and swim immediately, but do not fledge for another 7–8 weeks, during which they often fall victim to predators. One brood.
FEEDING: Feeds on a wide variety of aquatic foods, including animals and plants, usually by 'dabbling' with its head under water.

Like many species of duck, the female Mallard has a dull brown plumage, which enables her to remain inconspicuous while sitting on the nest, thus avoiding predators such as the fox.

The male Mallard is one of the most handsome of all our ducks, with his bottle-green head and dark magenta breast. Like most ducks, he goes through a period of moult in the summer.

SPARROWHAWK

Accipiter nisus Length 28–38 cm (11–15 in)

Blunt wings, long tail and powerful talons make the Sparrowhawk a formidable hunter, twisting and turning through the foliage in search of its songbird prey. Recent years have seen a major population increase, thanks to the banning of harmful agricultural chemicals such as DDT. Today, the Sparrowhawk is rapidly becoming the scourge of suburban bird-tables, though it must be remembered that unlike domestic cats, this magnificent bird is at least a natural predator.

IDENTIFICATION

Female larger than male: dark brown above, pale below, with dark mask through eye. Male blue-grey above, off-white tinted with orange below.

Usually seen in flight, where its short, rounded wings and long tail distinguish it from the slimmer, longer-winged Kestrel. Generally flies fast and low, alternating a series of wingflaps with short glides, before plunging into trees or bushes. Call a high-pitched, chattering 'kew-kew-kew'.

Like most birds of prey, the male Sparrowhawk is smaller than the female, with a brighter plumage. With short, rounded wings and a long tail, he is perfectly adapted for hunting among the trees.

Sparrowhawks bathe frequently, in order to keep their plumage as neat and clean as possible. This young bird has chosen a pond deep in the heart of a wood.

IN THE GARDEN

STATUS AND HABITAT: Increasingly common, especially in gardens with plenty of thick vegetation for the bird to conceal itself. In good weather will often soar high into the sky on stiff, broad wings.

BREEDING: Breeds from April to July, building loose nest from twigs, in a tree or bush. Lays 3–6 eggs, pale bluish-white with brownish blotches, and incubates for 4–5 weeks. Young fledge after 3–4 weeks. One brood in a season.

FEEDING: Feeds almost exclusively on small birds, especially Blue and Great Tits, taken in flight or from perch, after brief hunting flight. May sometimes be seen at 'plucking post', where it removes the feathers before eating.

COMMON BUZZARD

Buteo buteo Length 51–57 cm (20–22 in)

The largest bird of prey commonly seen in the British Isles, the Buzzard is a familiar sight in upland areas of northern and western Britain. Watch for Buzzards as they soar into the sky on broad wings, using thermal air currents to stay aloft. Most likely to be seen during fine, warm weather, from mid-morning onwards. Like other raptors, the Buzzard population has recently recovered in strength after a decline caused by the use of pesticides.

IDENTIFICATION

Usually seen in flight, where its dark brown plumage, broad wings (often held in a shallow 'V'), and fan-shaped tail are distinctive. Beware the occasional bird with very pale underparts, which can be confusing. In flight, appears longer-winged than crows; larger and more 'eagle-like' than Sparrowhawk. When perched, look for all-brown plumage and powerful hooked bill. Often gives loud 'mewing' call in flight.

IN THE GARDEN

STATUS AND HABITAT: Unlikely to actually visit gardens, but Buzzards are a regular sight over hilly, wooded country in south-west England and Wales, north-west England and Scotland. Especially abundant in Devon, Cornwall and Wales, where it can often be seen over built-up areas. Is also now spreading eastwards, occasionally breeding as far east as Norfolk.

BREEDING: Breeds in trees or on cliffs, building a large nest from twigs.

FEEDING: Feeds mainly on small animals, such as rodents, as well as frogs, worms and insects. Will also take carrion.

Above: *Buzzards are usually seen in flight, soaring high over the countryside on their broad wings. In recent years, Buzzards have begun to spread out from their usual haunts, colonizing new areas.*

Left: *Britain's largest common bird of prey, the Buzzard is rarely seen on the ground. A close-up view reveals the powerful, hooked beak and the feathering around the legs, a characteristic of large birds of prey.*

KESTREL

Falco tinnunculus Length 32–36 cm (13–14 in)

A hovering Kestrel is one of the great miracles of nature, hanging motionless in the sky before plummeting down onto its unsuspecting prey, a habit which earned the species the folk-name 'windhover'. Kestrels are equally at home in urban or rural surroundings, although they generally prefer to hunt in the open, therefore visiting gardens less often than their close relative the Sparrowhawk.

IDENTIFICATION

Male has grey head, rusty-orange back spotted with black, dark wingtips and tail. Underparts pale buff with dark streaks. Female larger and stockier, with streaked reddish-brown upperparts and buffish underparts, also streaked dark. Most often seen in flight, where its long, narrow, pointed wings distinguish it from the broader-winged Sparrowhawk. When perched, upright posture and slim build are distinctive. Call a sharp, high-pitched 'kee-kee-kee-kee'.

The Kestrel is our commonest bird of prey, a familiar sight as it perches on fenceposts and wires, or hovers in search of its quarry. It has adapted well to an urban existence, living alongside people in towns and cities.

IN THE GARDEN

STATUS AND HABITAT: Kestrels may fly over almost any garden, and often perch on roofs or in trees. Less frequently, a pair may take up territory, especially in larger gardens or near open land suitable for hunting.

BREEDING: Breeds from March to July in a variety of sites, including tree-holes or even on the roofs of buildings. Lays 3–6 eggs, pale with heavy reddish-brown blotches, and incubates for 4 weeks. Young fledge after 4–5 weeks. Sometimes uses specialized nestboxes. One brood.

FEEDING: Feeds mainly on voles, but will also take small birds, insects and even frogs.

The male is smaller and slimmer than the female, and has a bluish-grey head, black moustaches, and rufous back spotted with black. Kestrels nest in a variety of sites, including the roofs of buildings or in holes in trees.

PHEASANT

Phasianus colchicus Length 52–90 cm (20–35 in)

The Pheasant is one of our commonest birds, mainly because birds are artificially reared for shooting. However, as a garden visitor it is mainly confined to well-wooded, rural areas. Originally introduced to the British Isles, almost certainly by the Romans, it has since spread to most parts of the country. Can be surprisingly tame, sometimes even visiting bird tables, especially in hard weather.

IDENTIFICATION

Male unmistakable, with deep, rich russet-toned plumage, red-and-green head-pattern and long, plumed tail. Some males show white ring around neck. Female smaller than male, with plain brownish plumage and shorter tail, although the colour of both males and females may vary considerably. In flight, short, whirring wings and long tail distinctive. Call a deep, explosive croaking sound.

IN THE GARDEN

STATUS AND HABITAT: An increasingly frequent visitor to gardens in rural and semi-rural areas, due to a surplus of birds being raised for sport. Prefers to keep close to dense cover, such as shrubs and bushes.

BREEDING: Breeds from March to August, nesting on the ground, usually in long vegetation on the edges of woodlands. Lays large clutches of 8–15 pale greenish eggs, although sometimes as many as 20. Incubates for 3–4 weeks. Young fledge after 12–14 days, though are active as soon as they hatch. Generally polygynous (one male mates with several females). One brood.

FEEDING: Feeds on shoots of arable crops, though young mainly eat insects.

Above: *In contrast to the male, the female Pheasant is an inconspicuous, dull brown bird. She may lay up to 20 eggs, which she hides deep in the grass.*

Right: *With his red and green head pattern and deep russet plumage, the male Pheasant is one of our most handsome birds. Like other gamebirds, it generally feeds on the ground, where it searches for grain.*

MOORHEN

Gallinula chloropus Length 31–35 cm (12–14 in)

An unassuming bird, the Moorhen is easily overlooked, yet its behaviour and plumage make it one of our most attractive waterbirds. Distinguished from its close relative the Coot by a red-and-yellow pattern on bill, rather than white. Unlike the Coot, it frequently feeds away from water, on damp grassy areas such as lawns, so is a regular visitor to gardens near suitable habitat.

Above: *Like its close relative the Coot, the Moorhen spends a lot of time on the water, swimming in a characteristic jerky fashion, and dabbling beneath the surface with its colourful bill.*

Left: *Seen in close-up, the Moorhen is an attractive bird, with blackish-brown plumage contrasting with the red and yellow bill, and a distinctive flash of white beneath its tail.*

IDENTIFICATION

A medium-sized waterbird superficially resembling a small duck, although actually a member of the rail family. Plumage basically dark, shading subtly from sepia-brown above to purplish-black below, and divided by a broken white line running from shoulder to tail. Distinctive white flash on undertail, most obvious when bird is out of the water. Bill and frontal shield bright red, with yellow tip. Legs and feet greenish-yellow; feet large and unwebbed. Juveniles duller and paler brown. Call a variety of quiet clucks and louder, more strident notes.

IN THE GARDEN

STATUS AND HABITAT: Most frequently seen in gardens near lakes or ponds, with longish, damp grass where the birds can feed. May also visit gardens during hard winter weather, when usual sources of water are iced over.

BREEDING: Breeds by or on water, particularly reedbeds and ponds with sheltered vegetation, building a floating nest. Unlikely to breed in most gardens.

FEEDING: Feeds on a variety of small invertebrates, taken by dabbling in water or from land.

BLACK-HEADED GULL

Larus ridibundus Length 35–38 cm (14–15 in)

A noisy, sociable bird, the Black-headed Gull is now a familiar sight in both urban and rural areas, thanks to its ability to live alongside people. A century ago the situation was very different, with the species quite rare away from the sea. Today, it is by far our commonest and most widespread gull in inland areas, especially during the autumn and winter, when numbers are boosted by birds from the north and east.

IDENTIFICATION

A small, dove-like gull, with pearl-grey wings and white underparts. The black head (on closer inspection, actually a brown hood) is only present in breeding adults. The species is therefore more likely to be seen in non-breeding plumage: with a white head, apart from a dark smudge behind the eye. Wings tipped with black. Legs red or orange-red; bill red with dark tip. Juveniles show varying amounts of brown on wings. Makes a wide variety of loud, harsh calls, and can be very vocal.

IN THE GARDEN

STATUS AND HABITAT: Frequent visitor to gardens, sometimes in large and noisy flocks. Black-headed

In breeding plumage, the Black-headed Gull shows the distinctive dark hood that gives the species its name. A closer look reveals the colour to be chocolate-brown, rather than black.

Gulls often perch on rooftops, before dropping down to snatch food from lawns and bird tables. Commoner during the autumn and winter months, when large numbers move inland to take advantage of easy pickings in towns and cities.

BREEDING: Breeds in large colonies on sites away from gardens.

FEEDING: Very much an opportunistic feeder, eating almost anything, including kitchen scraps, stale bread and other household waste.

In autumn and winter, the Black-headed Gull loses its dark hood, though it retains a dark smudge around the eye. A sociable bird, it is often seen in quite large flocks.

COMMON GULL

Larus canus Length 38–43 cm (15–17 in)

A medium-sized, rather handsome gull, the only species other than Black-headed likely to visit gardens away from the sea. Despite its name, the Common Gull comes second to the Black-headed Gulls in abundance over most of the country. However, it can usually be found in small numbers, often among mixed gull flocks, where its plumper shape, larger size and more upright posture distinguish it from its black-headed relative.

IDENTIFICATION

Noticeably larger and plumper than Black-headed Gull, with deeper grey back and wings and all-white head and underparts. In winter, head may be flecked with dark, greyish streaks. Young birds show variable amounts of brown on wings and back. Legs greenish-yellow; bill yellowish with variable dark ring near tip. In flight, wings appear more rounded in shape than the pointed wings of Black-headed Gull. Call a loud, mewing sound.

The rounded wings, with black wingtips contrasting with grey, give the Common Gull a distinctive appearance, especially when seen in flight.

IN THE GARDEN

STATUS AND HABITAT: Although not present in such large numbers as the Black-headed Gull, the Common Gull is a widespread and regular autumn and winter visitor to many inland areas of the British Isles. Shyer, and rather less inclined to visit gardens than its smaller relative, it will nevertheless sometimes visit bird tables in search of food.

BREEDING: Breeds in large colonies away from gardens.

FEEDING: Eats a wide variety of food, ranging from natural prey to kitchen scraps, stale bread, etc.

Larger and plumper than Black-headed, the Common Gull is a fairly widespread and common winter visitor, which may visit gardens in search of easy pickings.

85

FERAL PIGEON

Columba livia Length 31–34 cm (12–13 in)

Descended from the wild Rock Dove of our remote northern coasts, the Feral (otherwise known as 'London' or 'Domestic') Pigeon is probably the most successful urban species of bird in the world. In some towns and cities the Feral Pigeon is so abundant that it has become an unwelcome pest. The northward spread of the species is now beginning to threaten the purity of its wild ancestors.

IDENTIFICATION

Feral Pigeons come in a wide variety of colours and plumage patterns, from the 'classic' black and grey, through brown, to almost pure white. Typical birds closely resemble their wild ancestors, with dark grey head, pale grey body, dark patches on the wings, a purplish throat and a greenish patch on the neck. However, birds may show variable amounts of white, buff and brown, in a whole range of bizarre patterns. They often have a white patch on the rump that is noticeable in flight. They frequently fly in flocks, with an effortless, gliding style. Call is a wide variety of throaty, cooing notes.

IN THE GARDEN

STATUS AND HABITAT: A common and familiar garden visitor, especially in urban and suburban areas, where it forms large flocks, often perching on roofs.
BREEDING: When food is plentiful the species can breed all year round, raising as many as six broods. Lays 2 white eggs, and incubates for 16–19 days. Young fledge after 4–5 weeks, and are able to breed themselves as early as 6 months old.
FEEDING: Feeds on almost anything – frequently getting food indirectly or directly from a human source. Will also eat large quantities of seeds.

Above: *A noisy, sociable bird, Feral Pigeons come in a wide range of colours and shades, as shown by this flock of bathing birds. Their variety derives from domestic breeding.*

Left: *Love them or hate them, it is impossible to ignore Feral Pigeons, one of our most common and familiar urban birds. Flocks frequently gather to feed on food provided by people, especially in cities.*

STOCK DOVE

Columba oenas Length 32–34 cm (13 in)

Although widespread, this is a shy, elusive dove, more often present than actually seen. Stock Doves are most obvious in early spring, when pairs perform their spectacular display-flight from a high perch on a tree, clapping their wings and soaring in circles together. Most likely to be seen in rural or suburban gardens, with plenty of large, mature trees for the birds to roost and breed.

IDENTIFICATION

Superficially resembles a small Woodpigeon, although can be told apart by smaller size, more delicate appearance, and lack of white on neck and wing. Plumage basically dark grey, with greenish patch on neck, pink shading on upper breast, and dark tips to wings. Bill yellow, legs pinkish. In flight looks stockier and shorter-tailed than Woodpigeon, with grey and black wing-pattern. In late summer and autumn beware confusion with juvenile Woodpigeons, which lack the adults' white collar. Call a repetitive, disyllabic cooing.

Smaller and shyer than their close relative the Woodpigeon, Stock Doves are a widespread but easily overlooked resident throughout the British Isles, and may be seen in rural or suburban gardens.

The yellow base to the bill, greenish sheen on the neck, and lack of white collar and wingbars are the best ways to tell the Stock Dove apart from the commoner Wood and Feral Pigeons.

IN THE GARDEN

STATUS AND HABITAT: Most likely to be seen in rural or suburban gardens, especially those near well-wooded parkland. Found throughout England and Wales, and in southern Scotland and Ireland. With patience, will allow close and prolonged views.
BREEDING: Breeds from February to November, usually in a hole in a tree, but will sometimes use nestboxes. Lays 2 white eggs, and incubates for 16–18 days. Young fledge after 3–4 weeks. Like other pigeons, Stock Doves are multiple-brooded, with up to five broods recorded in a single season.
FEEDING: Feeds mainly on seeds, generally taken from the ground.

WOODPIGEON

Columba palumbus Length 40–42 cm (16 in)

One of our most familiar large garden birds, the Woodpigeon is found throughout Britain and Ireland, in rural areas, suburbs and even in the heart of cities. With its catholic taste in food, roosting and nesting places, it is rapidly becoming almost as adaptable and widespread as its cousin the Feral Pigeon. Woodpigeons have been known to lay eggs in almost every month of the year – one explanation for the success of the species!

IDENTIFICATION

Our largest pigeon or dove, always appearing noticeably bigger and bulkier than other pigeons. Upperparts mid-grey, with lighter edge to wings. Chest purplish-pink, shading to pale grey on belly. Head grey, with obvious white patch on side of neck (lacking in young birds). Bill, legs and feet yellow. Tail has broad dark band across tip. In flight, shows obvious white line across centre of wing. Song, the familiar, repetitive 'coo-COO, coo, coo-coo', with the emphasis on the second syllable.

Observed in close-up, the variety of colours and shades in the Woodpigeon's plumage can be seen, ranging from grey, through mauve, to a delicate pink on the breast.

IN THE GARDEN

STATUS AND HABITAT: A regular visitor to most gardens, often feeding on open lawns. Also perches on bushes and trees, sometimes even hanging from small twigs to feed on berries.

BREEDING: Breeds almost all year round, even building nests and laying eggs in the middle of winter, although the main breeding season is from June to September. Normally lays 2 white eggs, and incubates for 16–17 days. Young fledge after 3–5 weeks. Usually raises two broods, depending on available food.

FEEDING: Feeds on plants: especially shoots, seeds and berries. Will frequently feed on the ground beneath feeders and bird-tables, picking up the spilled seed.

The Woodpigeon is a common and familiar garden visitor, frequently feeding on the lawn beneath bird tables, where it can pick up spilled nuts or seeds. The large size and white collar are distinctive.

COLLARED DOVE

Streptopelia decaocto Length 31–33 cm (12–13 in)

Today the Collared Dove is such a familiar garden bird that it is hard to believe that half a century ago the species was unknown in the British Isles. Since first colonizing north-west Europe in the 1950s, it has spread far and wide, and today its gentle, monotonous cooing is a familiar sound throughout the region. An attractive species, it is a welcome addition to the birdlife of our towns and gardens.

IDENTIFICATION

A slim, medium-sized dove, with a predominantly pinkish-buff plumage. The neck ring, which gives the bird its name is black, edged with white. Wings tipped with black. In flight, whitish tips to tail-feathers and black wingtips contrast with pale brown body. Song a three-syllable 'coooo-COOOO-coo', with the stress on the middle syllable, and the final syllable more abrupt.

IN THE GARDEN

STATUS AND HABITAT: A common resident, especially in towns, villages and suburbs, though much less frequent in urban areas. Often perches on telegraph poles, TV aerials and roofs, where it gives its repetitive call.

BREEDING: Breeds mainly between February and October, although eggs have been recorded in every month of the year. Lays 2 white eggs, and incubates for 14–18 days. Young fledge after 2–3 weeks. Collared Doves will even lay a new clutch while still feeding chicks, and five broods in a single season is not unknown. No wonder they have spread so quickly!

FEEDING: Feeds mainly on grains, often taken from the surplus on farms.

The Collared Dove, as its name suggests, sports a distinctive black ring, edged with white, around the neck. Its pinkish-buff plumage and delicate build are also distinctive.

Our most successful recent colonist, the Collared Dove is now a familiar garden visitor throughout most of the British Isles, regularly visiting bird tables.

TURTLE DOVE

Streptopelia turtur Length 26–28 cm (10–11 in)

The smallest European pigeon or dove, and our only summer migrant pigeon species, the Turtle Dove returns north in late April and early May to breed. In recent years it has undergone a rapid decline in numbers, owing to a combination of drought in its African winter quarters and changes in farming practices in Britain. Nevertheless, the Turtle Dove's purring song, from which the species gets its name, is still one of the classic sounds of summer.

IDENTIFICATION

A slim, long-tailed dove, with a delicately marked plumage. Can be told apart from its larger relative the Collared Dove by smaller size and darker appearance. Has 'scalloped' pattern on wings, with dark centres to orange feathers and dark wingtips. Head, neck and underparts dusky pink, with distinctive black-and-white striped collar on sides and back of neck. Short legs give distinctive horizontal gait when seen on ground. In flight, small size and all-dark underwings distinguish it from Collared Dove. Song a repetitive, deep, rhythmic purring.

IN THE GARDEN

STATUS AND HABITAT: Summer visitor, from late April or early May to August or September. Found mainly in rural areas in the south and east of Britain, though now absent from many of its former haunts.
BREEDING: Breeds from May to August, building nest from sticks in bush or tree, especially hawthorn or elder. Lays 1 or 2 white eggs, and incubates for 13–14 days. Young fledge after about 3 weeks. Normally raises two, sometimes even three, broods in a season.
FEEDING: During the breeding season feeds almost exclusively on weed seeds – the scarcity of which may be partly responsible for the species' recent decline.

Above: *Britain's smallest and most attractive species of pigeon or dove, the Turtle Dove is a summer visitor to Europe. It travels south in the autumn to spend the winter on the African continent.*

Left: *Like many migrants, the Turtle Dove has recently undergone a spectacular and rapid decline. However it is a regular summer visitor to Britain, often building a discreet nest in pine trees.*

RING-NECKED (ROSE-RINGED) PARAKEET

Psittacula krameri Length 38–42 cm (15–17 in)

This spectacular addition to our garden list was first recorded in the wild during the late 1960s and early 1970s, when captive birds escaped or were deliberately released in the Home Counties. Since then, this Asian exotic has become a familiar though still localized visitor to gardens in various parts of southern England. The Ring-necked Parakeet's adaptability, high breeding success and ability to survive harsh winter weather are likely to lead to even greater success.

IDENTIFICATION

Unmistakable! With its bright, emerald-green plumage, long tail and piercing call, the Ring-necked Parakeet is unique among our garden birds. Told apart from other escaped parrots by red bill and black collar, edged with pink, although this neckband is lacking on the juvenile. In flight shows pointed wings with rapid, shallow beats, and very long tail. When perched can be surprisingly difficult to see, as the green plumage provides excellent camouflage in the trees. Makes a variety of calls, mostly high-pitched screeching noises, reminiscent of Green Woodpecker.

IN THE GARDEN

STATUS AND HABITAT: Very locally distributed in south-east England, mainly in the London suburbs and Home Counties. Regularly visits garden bird-tables, especially in winter, and will readily perch on artificial feeders.

BREEDING: Breeds from January to June, nesting in cavities, especially holes in trees, where it competes with other hole-nesters such as Kestrel, Stock Dove and Jackdaw. Lays 2–4 white eggs, and incubates for 22–24 days. Young fledge after 6–7 weeks. One, perhaps two, broods.

FEEDING: Feeds mainly on soft fruit, although in winter will happily take peanuts and other food provided by man.

Originally from northern India, this brightly-coloured and raucous-sounding parakeet was first introduced into south-east England during the 1970s. Males show the black and pink collar which gives the bird its name.

Ring-necked Parakeets nest in holes in trees, often competing with other hole-nesters for space. They will alert you to their presence by loud screeching.

CUCKOO

Cuculus canorus Length 32–34 cm (13 in)

The Cuckoo's onomatopoeic call is the classic sound of summer across the whole of Europe. Indeed, the bird's arrival in spring has for long been the subject of folklore, letters to national newspapers and hoaxes by small boys. The Cuckoo is also famous for its habit of brood-parasitism, or laying its eggs in other birds nests. Although its call is all-pervasive, the bird itself can be surprisingly difficult to see.

IDENTIFICATION

A long-winged, long-tailed, hawk-like bird, easily mistaken in flight for a falcon or Sparrowhawk. When perched, distinctive horizontal posture with tail held up. Upperparts, head, neck and throat steel-grey. Underparts closely barred black and white. Can also occur in brownish-red plumage phase. Male's song unmistakable. Female has low, bubbling call.

IN THE GARDEN

STATUS AND HABITAT: Summer visitor to rural areas, from late April or early May until July–August, though can be difficult to find after males stop

The familiar two-note call of the Cuckoo heralds the coming of spring throughout the region. A secretive bird, the Cuckoo is best-known for its habit of laying its eggs in other birds nests, leaving them to raise its young.

singing in June. Commonest where host species, such as Meadow Pipit, Dunnock, Reed Warbler and Pied Wagtail, are found.

BREEDING: Lays a single egg in between 6 and 25 different nests, often imitating the host's egg to avoid detection. Female Cuckoos remove one of the host's eggs before laying their own. Young hatch after 11–13 days, and immediately begin to eject other eggs and chicks from the nest. After being fed constantly by the unsuspecting host parents, the single Cuckoo chick fledges after 17–21 days, though often continues to be fed for some time after leaving the nest.

FEEDING: Mainly feeds on hairy caterpillars.

The young Cuckoo soon outgrows the nest of its smaller host species – in this case the Reed Warbler. This bird is waiting for the unsuspecting host parents to return with food.

BARN OWL

Tyto alba Length 33–39 cm (13–15 in)

The Barn Owl, as its name suggests, is closely linked to farming activities, often building its nest in a working barn. As it goes forth to hunt on the evening air, the Barn Owl's pale white plumage and silent flight give it a mysterious, ghostly appearance. Its loud, piercing call has given the species the alternative country name of Screech Owl.

IDENTIFICATION

A medium-sized, very pale owl, often appearing almost completely white in flight. Upperparts in fact pale yellowish-buff, delicately marked with small bluish spots. Underparts and underwings white. Face heart-shaped, with piercing, forward-facing eyes bordered by a thin grey line. Flies on long, broad, rounded wings, often held in a shallow 'V' as the owl glides low over the ground in search of food.

The decline in traditional farming means that there are fewer natural nest-sites available for the Barn Owl to breed. Many farmers have compensated for this by providing artificial nestboxes in new barns.

Mainly nocturnal, although will often hunt at dawn and dusk, especially during the winter. Call a loud, piercing screech.

IN THE GARDEN

STATUS AND HABITAT: Barn Owls are closely tied to lowland farms, and are only likely to occur in or near large gardens in rural farming areas. Because they hunt by flying low over the ground, they are often hit by moving vehicles, so are more commonly seen away from major roads.

BREEDING: Breeds mainly in large buildings, often in barns. Lays 4–7 white eggs, and incubates them for 4–5 weeks. Young fledge after 7–12 weeks. Produces one, sometimes two, broods. In recent years, has been greatly helped by the provision of artificial nestboxes.

FEEDING: Feeds mainly on rodents, especially voles, caught by hunting in low flight.

Like most owls, the Barn Owl is mainly nocturnal, though it often hunts in the hours after dawn or before dusk, quartering low over the ground in search of its favourite food, voles.

LITTLE OWL

Athene noctua Length 21–23 cm (8–9 in)

The smallest and most diurnal of our owls, often seen perched on a prominent post, roof or wire. Since it was introduced to southern England during the nineteenth century, the Little Owl has spread throughout much of lowland Britain. Today this delightful bird is a frequent and characteristic sight, especially in areas of mixed farming.

IDENTIFICATION

Barely the length of a Song Thrush, its tiny size, spotted plumage and bright yellow eyes make the Little Owl relatively easy to identify. More often seen during the day than other owls, although most active around dawn and dusk. Mainly greyish-brown, with bold white spots on back, wings and underparts, and finer white streaks on crown. Face pale, with typical mask-like appearance and staring yellow eyes. Legs long, and covered in feathers. Flight undulating, with large head, dumpy body and round wings. Often sings and calls from perch, making a wide variety of yelping and piercing noises.

Unlike most British owls, the Little Owl is frequently seen during the day, often perched on a tree, fencepost or building. It feeds on a wide variety of food, including small mammals, insects and baby birds.

The Little Owl is not a native British bird, having been introduced into parts of southern Britain during the nineteenth century, mainly by aristocratic landowners.

IN THE GARDEN

STATUS AND HABITAT: Found mainly in lowland, rural areas of southern and eastern Britain. Occasionally visits gardens from nearby farmland.

BREEDING: Breeds from March to September, usually nesting in cavities in buildings or holes in trees. Lays 3–5 white eggs, and incubates for 3–4 weeks. Young leave the nest after 4–5 days, though do not fledge for another 3 weeks or so, and often remain with parents for some time afterwards. Single brooded.

FEEDING: Feeds on small mammals, birds, insects and other invertebrates.

TAWNY OWL

Strix aluco Length 37–39 cm (15 in)

Our commonest and most widespread owl, yet because of its mainly nocturnal lifestyle, the Tawny Owl is far more frequently heard than seen. Its famous hooting call is a familiar night-time sound throughout rural and suburban Britain, especially in late winter and early spring. Occasionally a Tawny Owl may be discovered at a daytime roost, where it can allow a very close approach.

Like other owls, the Tawny Owl's eyes face forward, giving it binocular vision. To compensate, its flexible neck allows it to turn its head from side to side to keep watch for any threat.

Despite being widespread throughout Britain, its nocturnal habits mean that the Tawny Owl can often be difficult to see. It hunts on silent wings, searching for rodents, which it seizes with its sharp talons.

IDENTIFICATION

Medium-sized, rather plump owl, with mainly brown plumage, though this can vary from grey to rufous in tone. Dark centres to feathers give mottled, streaked appearance. At night, may be seen as only a ghostly silhouette as it flies between trees or perches on a branch. A Tawny Owl's presence is usually given away by sound, including the classic 'tu-whit, to-whoo' song. Also gives high-pitched 'kee-wick' call.

IN THE GARDEN

STATUS AND HABITAT: Tawny Owls are highly sedentary, staying on their territories throughout the year, even during the harshest winter weather. Most often found in gardens near mixed or deciduous woodland, or with plenty of mature trees in which the owls can breed and roost. Owls are often discovered in the early months of the year, when they are most vocal. Found throughout Britain, but absent from Ireland.

BREEDING: Breeds from March to August, nesting in holes in large trees. Lays 2–5 all-white eggs, and incubates for 28–30 days. Young fledge after about 5 weeks, but often leave the nest earlier than this. One brood in a season.

FEEDING: Wide choice of diet: mainly rodents, but also takes amphibians, birds and even insects, when severe weather means that food is scarce.

SWIFT

Apus apus Length 16–17 cm (6–7 in)

One of the most familiar summer sounds of the city is the screaming of Swifts, as they chase each other in flocks across the sky. The Swift is without doubt the perfect flying machine, cutting through the air on scythe-like wings and torpedo-shaped body. Swifts live almost all their life airborne, feeding, courting and even sleeping on the wing.

IDENTIFICATION

Although often confused with the Swallow or House Martin, the Swift is in fact highly distinctive. Its cigar-shaped body, long, scythe-like wings and sooty-brown plumage (appearing black at a distance) make identification relatively simple. Given close views, the pale edges to the wings, pale throat and shallow fork to the tail are apparent. Call: a piercing scream, often delivered as a joint chorus in a communal flight just before dusk.

The Swift is the most aerial of all our birds, spending almost its entire life airborne. It feeds exclusively on flying insects, which it snatches on the wing.

by mid-May, but in wet springs not until June. Nests in colonies, usually in roofs of buildings. Lays 2–3 white eggs, which hatch between 19 and 27 days later, depending on the weather and available food. Young fledge after 5–8 weeks, again depending on the weather.

FEEDING: Feeds exclusively on small flying insects, always taken in flight.

IN THE GARDEN

STATUS AND HABITAT: Swifts are a common summer visitor throughout most of Britain. The first birds return in late April or early May, though the main arrival is usually a week or two later. During May and June they are continually present, except when bad weather forces them to flee for a day or two, when the chicks become torpid in order to survive without food. By July the birds begin to head south, and are rarely seen after August.

BREEDING: Breeds as soon as the weather is warm enough to provide enough flying insects; sometimes

Swifts breed in the roofs of buildings, where they build a simple nest from grass and feathers. The chicks are often left unattended for long periods, especially during bad weather, when the parents are forced to flee.

KINGFISHER

Alcedo atthis Length 16–17 cm (6–7 in)

A sudden, blinding flash of blue and orange signals the arrival of a Kingfisher at your garden pond. This stunningly colourful bird is the perfect fishing machine, plunging under the water before emerging with its catch in its powerful bill. Kingfishers are only an occasional visitor to gardens, and if you are lucky enough to see one it will be an unforgettable experience.

IDENTIFICATION

Unmistakable! A tiny jewel of a bird, barely larger than a sparrow. Crown and upperparts bright turquoise-blue, darker on wings. Cheeks and underparts deep russet-orange, throat white. Female has orange on lower bill. When seen in flight, plumage flashes blue and orange as the bird turns to catch the light. A shy bird, often heard before it is seen: a loud, piercing, high-pitched call, which carries for long distances.

IN THE GARDEN

STATUS AND HABITAT: Most likely to be seen in gardens with a well-stocked fishpond, or those adjacent to a lake, river or stream. Kingfishers are wary of humans, so often visit early in the morning. During hard winter weather, when they are forced to seek unfrozen water to feed, they often turn up in unexpected places.

BREEDING: Breeds from March to September, in a hole, usually situated in a soft, exposed sandbank alongside water. Lays 5–7 white eggs, and incubates for 19–20 days. Young fledge after 3–4 weeks. Usually two, sometimes three, broods.

FEEDING: Feeds on fish and aquatic invertebrates, mostly taken by plunging into the water.

Kingfishers often visit garden ponds in search of easy pickings, especially in the hour or two after sunrise. Look out for a sudden flash of blue and orange which signals its presence.

A fabulous jewel of a bird, shy and wary of approach by humans. You may be fortunate enough to catch sight of one sat on a perch, like this one, with a freshly caught fish in its bill.

HOOPOE

Upupa epops Length 26–28 cm (10–11 in)

Cross the Channel, head south, and you'll soon come across one of Europe's most striking and beautiful birds: the Hoopoe. Despite being widespread on the near continent, the Hoopoe is a rare visitor to the British Isles, mostly appearing in southern England during fine weather in early spring. Occasionally, in warm summers, a pair will stay to breed, although if global warming continues, this may become a more regular occurrence.

Above: *Despite its bright pink plumage, black-and-white wings and extraordinary crest, the Hoopoe is a shy bird, often seen only in flight. During the breeding season Hoopoes make the far-carrying call which gives the species its name.*

Left: *Like many birds, Hoopoes prefer to bathe in dust rather than water. This bird has ruffled up its plumage in order to remove surplus oil and parasites from its feathers.*

IDENTIFICATION

With its extraordinary crest, deep orange-pink plumage and black-and-white wing-pattern, the Hoopoe is surely unmistakable. In flight, on rounded wings, it looks more like a giant butterfly than a bird. On the ground, however, it can be surprisingly elusive and hard to see. Listen out for the extraordinary call which gives the species its name: a deep, penetrating 'hoo-hoo-hoo'.

IN THE GARDEN

STATUS AND HABITAT: Hoopoes are most frequently seen in traditional farming areas, where they regularly visit gardens, especially if there are open areas for feeding, and hollow trees in which they can build a nest. It is a summer visitor, usually arriving in April and leaving in September or October.

BREEDING: Breeds from April to July, building its nest in a hole in a tree or building. Lays 5–8 yellowish-olive eggs, and incubates for 15–19 days. Young fledge after 3–4 weeks. Usually one brood, although two sometimes recorded.

FEEDING: Feeds mainly on insects and their larvae, which are caught on the ground or by probing and extracting the larvae from the soft earth with its long bill. Sometimes takes lizards.

WRYNECK

Jynx torquilla Length 16–17 cm (6–6.5 in)

One of Europe's most peculiar birds, the Wryneck has undergone a long decline in the north-west of its range, and is now extinct as a British breeding bird. However, it is still widespread in continental Europe north to Scandinavia, where it is a regular if sometimes elusive visitor to gardens. Its bizarre plumage and strange habits make it appear almost reptilian, rather than bird-like.

IDENTIFICATION

Related to the woodpeckers, although quite unlike them in shape and coloration. On first sighting, the Wryneck appears to be just another dull, brown bird. However, a closer look reveals a plumage of extraordinary complexity: a mixture of greys, browns and blacks, with patterns of bars, spots and subtle shading, almost like the bark of a tree. Body long, with a large head and plump belly. More often heard than seen: its call a plaintive and repetitive 'tu-tu-tu-tu-tu', reminiscent of Kestrel or Hobby.

IN THE GARDEN

STATUS AND HABITAT: The Wryneck is a woodland bird, well suited to parks and gardens, especially well-wooded ones. As a hole-nester, it will readily adapt to using nestboxes. Summer visitor, arriving April–May, and leaving August–October.
BREEDING: Breeds from April to August, nesting in a hole in a tree (often taking over a disused woodpecker's nest). Lays 6–11 white eggs, and incubates for 11–14 days. Young fledge after 18–22 days. Occasionally two, sometimes three, broods.

Although closely related to the woodpeckers, at first sight the Wryneck looks more like a thrush or chat. However, a closer look reveals the extraordinary plumage, with its complex pattern of blacks, browns and greys.

FEEDING: Feeds mainly on ants, using its long, sticky tongue. Will also take other small insects. Often feeds on the ground.

Although still fairly common and widespread in continental Europe, the Wryneck has undergone a spectacular decline in the British Isles, and is now extinct as a British breeding bird.

GREEN WOODPECKER

Picus viridis Length 31–33 cm (12–13 in)

Of our three native species of woodpecker, the Green is the only one to feed regularly on the ground, where it will search for its favourite food, ants. When disturbed, flees with deliberate, undulating flight, often giving its characteristic laughing call, which earned the species the folk-name the 'Yaffle'. In many places it also has a reputation for bringing rain, hence another country name – the 'rain bird'.

IDENTIFICATION

By far our largest woodpecker, the size of a Feral Pigeon. Green-and-yellow plumage, red on head and black 'highwayman's mask' are distinctive. Upperparts yellowish-green, with dark grey wingtips. Underparts pale buffish-yellow. Crown scarlet; black mask around eyes. Heavy, powerful beak. In flight, broad wings and yellow rump obvious. Often heard rather than seen: the call is a repeated, high-pitched single note, which really does sound like ringing laughter.

Green Woodpeckers feed mainly on ants, which they dig up from short, cropped grass - so the species is a regular visitor to larger gardens. However, it is a shy bird, so don't go too close! This bird is a juvenile.

The far-carrying, laughing call of the Green Woodpecker is often heard before the bird is seen. Our largest woodpecker, its yellow-green plumage, red crown and black facial stripes are very distinctive.

IN THE GARDEN

STATUS AND HABITAT: Found in rural and suburban gardens with large, mature trees, and wide open lawns, especially near parkland. Often feeds in the open, digging into the ground for ants. May also be seen perched on the side of a tree in the usual woodpecker manner. However, unlike other woodpeckers, rarely drums. Not found in Ireland, and rare in most of Scotland.

BREEDING: Breeds from March to June, nesting in a hole excavated in a tree. Lays 5–7 white eggs, and incubates for 17–19 days. Young fledge after 18–21 days. One brood.

FEEDING: Feeds almost exclusively on ants taken from the ground, using its long, sticky tongue.

GREAT SPOTTED WOODPECKER

Dendrocopos major Length 22–23 cm (9 in)

Our commonest and most widespread woodpecker, found in a wide variety of wooded habitats, including gardens. Most often seen while feeding on a tree-trunk or branch in classic woodpecker fashion, in search of grubs and insects. Like other woodpeckers, it has a specially adapted beak, head and neck to allow it to perform its extraordinary 'drumming'.

IDENTIFICATION

A medium-sized woodpecker, slightly larger than a Starling. Male and female share distinctive black-and-white plumage. Upperparts mainly black, with large, white, oval patches on wings and black-and-white barring on flight feathers. Underparts dirty-white, with bright cherry-red patch on belly beneath the tail. Head pattern of black bars surrounding white cheeks. Male distinguished by red patch on rear of crown. Deliberate, undulating flight. Drums far more often than other woodpeckers, especially in early spring when establishing a territory. Calls often: a loud, metallic 'chip', either given singly or repeated.

Great Spotted Woodpeckers feed mainly on branches and trunks of trees, probing beneath the bark with their stout and powerful bill, in search of wood-boring insects. In winter they will also visit bird tables.

With its striking black-and-white plumage and red beneath the tail, the Great Spotted Woodpecker is a handsome bird. The male also has a small patch of red on the back of his head, lacking in the female.

IN THE GARDEN

STATUS AND HABITAT: Found in many rural and suburban gardens, especially those with mature trees. In winter, ranges more widely, and will visit garden feeding-stations. Not found in Ireland.

BREEDING: Breeds from March to June, though drumming may begin as early as January. Nests in hole drilled in tree. Lays 4–7 white eggs, and incubates for 16 days. Young fledge after 18–24 days. One brood.

FEEDING: Feeds on insects, especially wood-boring ones found in the bark of trees. In winter will take food from bird-tables, with a preference for fat.

LESSER SPOTTED WOODPECKER

Dendrocopos minor Length 14–15 cm (6 in)

Our smallest woodpecker, barely the size of a sparrow. Lesser Spotted Woodpeckers are often overlooked, and may be present for some time in an area before they are seen. Often creeps silently among the branches of a tree, more like a songbird than a woodpecker, although once seen may give excellent views.

IDENTIFICATION

Tiny woodpecker, superficially similar to its larger relative the Great Spotted. Given good views, Lesser Spotted's smaller size, barring right across back and wings (lacking oval patches of Great Spotted), and lack of red on belly are distinctive. Male has more extensive red patch on top of crown; both sexes have pale forehead. Undulating flight. Drums more rarely than Great Spotted, and drumbeat quieter and less powerful. Call again like Great Spotted, but weaker; sometimes also makes a repetitive 'kee-kee-kee-kee-kee-kee' sound.

IN THE GARDEN

STATUS AND HABITAT: An uncommon and localized resident in rural areas of southern Britain, where may be found in large, quiet gardens with plenty of mature, broadleaved trees. Most likely to be seen during the late winter and early spring, before the leaves are out. Look for nest-holes high in trees – usually much higher than other woodpecker nests, and often on the underside of a small branch. Not found in Ireland or Scotland.

BREEDING: Breeds from March to June, nesting in specially dug hole in tree. Lays 4–6 white eggs, and incubates for 11–14 days. Young fledge after 18–21 days. One brood.

FEEDING: Feeds on grubs and insects, which it finds in small branches of trees.

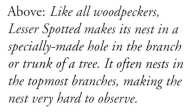

Above: *Like all woodpeckers, Lesser Spotted makes its nest in a specially-made hole in the branch or trunk of a tree. It often nests in the topmost branches, making the nest very hard to observe.*

Left: *Its small size and secretive habits make the Lesser Spotted Woodpecker easy to overlook. It tends to feed on smaller twigs and branches than its larger relative, probing for tiny insects beneath the bark.*

SWALLOW

Hirundo rustica Length 19–22 cm (7.5–9 in)

Throughout Europe, the coming of the first Swallow signals the end of the long northern winter, and the welcome arrival of spring – although as Shakespeare warned, "One Swallow doth not a summer make". Our most familiar summer visitor is found mainly in rural areas, hawking low over the ground for insects on long, graceful wings.

IDENTIFICATION

Usually seen in flight, where its long tail-streamers, all-dark upperparts, pale underparts and red throat set it apart from its closest relatives the martins, and from the unrelated Swift. At close range, upperparts are dark blue, shading to slate-grey on wings; underparts are creamy-white, with blue breast-band and brick-red throat. Tail long, with deep fork giving buoyant appearance in flight. Song a rapid, varied twittering, and delivered either when perched or on the wing. Call a lively 'chit'.

IN THE GARDEN

STATUS AND HABITAT: Found from April to September throughout Britain, though most common in lowland country districts near farmland, and generally absent from urban areas. Often perches on the roofs of buildings, or in flocks on telegraph wires, especially during late summer and early autumn. Flies low, hunting for insect prey.

BREEDING: Breeds from April to August, usually nesting in buildings, where it builds an open cup-shaped nest out of mud. Lays 4–5 eggs, white with red spots, and incubates for 14–16 days. Young fledge after about 3 weeks, and often help parents raise young from second, sometimes third, broods.

FEEDING: Feeds on flying insects, caught on the wing.

Above: *Our best-known summer migrant, the Swallow returns from its African winter quarters in April, heralding the arrival of spring. The long tail-streamers, deep blue upperparts and brick-red throat tell it apart from Swifts and martins.*

Right: *Swallows build a cup-shaped nest out of tiny balls of mud, usually in the eaves of a house or barn. This bird is collecting mud from a nearby puddle, to take back to the nest.*

HOUSE MARTIN

Delichon urbica Length 12.5 cm (5 in)

As both its English and scientific names suggest, the House Martin is a bird closely associated with towns and cities. Originally a cave-nester, it long ago adapted to live alongside people, building its nest under the eaves of houses. A colony of House Martins is supposed to bring good luck to the householder, although neighbours roused by the noise of hungry chicks might not agree!

IDENTIFICATION

A small, compact hirundine, easily distinguished from its relatives by its blue-black upperparts, white underparts, neat white rump and short tail. Most often seen in flight, where it hunts for insects on short, triangular wings. Often hunts high in the sky, alongside Swifts, especially on summer evenings when the weather is fine. Song is a scratchy, babbling twitter with a variety of notes; call a short, sharp 'prritt'.

IN THE GARDEN

STATUS AND HABITAT: House Martins return to Britain in late April or early May. They are familiar visitors to gardens in villages, towns and cities throughout the country, departing again for Africa in August or September. Often seen with Swallows on telegraph wires just prior to departure.

BREEDING: Breeds from May to August, building its characteristic semi-spherical nest out of tiny balls of mud under the eaves of houses. Lays 3–5 whitish eggs, and incubates for 14–16 days. Young fledge after 2–3 weeks. Two, sometimes three, broods.

FEEDING: Feeds mainly on insects, caught in flight.

Above: *House Martins like to be near water, both to catch flying insects and to collect copious amounts of mud needed for nest building.*

Right: *The House Martin is smaller and more compact than its close relative the Swallow, with dark blue upperparts contrasting with pure white underparts. It also builds a nest from mud, under the eaves of a house.*

YELLOW (BLUE-HEADED) WAGTAIL

Motacilla flava Length 17 cm (6.5 in)

One of our most graceful and colourful small birds, the Yellow Wagtail comes in a wide variety of races, generally told apart by their head colour. The British race has an olive and yellow head, whereas continental European birds have a blue head, and the Scandinavian form a grey head.

IDENTIFICATION

An elegant, delicate wagtail, with the typical long tail of its family. Throat and underparts bright sulphur-yellow; head and upperparts olive, darker on wings. Tail dark olive with white outer feathers. Told apart from Grey Wagtail by olive coloration and lack of grey and black in plumage. Juveniles dull buffish in colour, lacking most of yellow tones, and can sometimes be confused with young Pied Wagtails. Continental race (Blue-headed) has blue-grey head pattern, with white stripes through the eye and lower face; Scandinavian race (Grey-headed) has slate-grey head and face. Call a high-pitched 'tsee-eee'.

The continental race of the species is known as Blue-headed Wagtail, due to its distinctive bluish-grey head pattern, which contrasts with the olive-green upperparts and bright yellow underparts.

The British race of the Yellow Wagtail is one of our most handsome breeding birds, with bright sulphur-yellow head, neck and underparts and olive-green back and wings. It is a summer visitor to the British Isles, usually arriving back in April.

IN THE GARDEN

STATUS AND HABITAT: Summer visitor, returning in April or May, and usually departing in August or September. Is an uncommon but occasional visitor to gardens, especially during the spring or autumn, when migrants can turn up almost anywhere. Most likely to be seen near water.

BREEDING: Breeds in marshy areas, damp meadows and on farmland, away from gardens.

FEEDING: Feeds mainly on insects and also on other small invertebrates, which it catches in short, 'flycatching' flight or on the ground.

GREY WAGTAIL

Motacilla cinerea Length 18–19 cm (7–7.5 in)

With its bobbing gait, slender body and extraordinary tail, the Grey Wagtail is one of our most beautiful and elegant birds. Occasionally visits gardens near water, especially in upland areas, where it favours fast-flowing rivers and streams. Despite its name, the plumage is mainly yellow, especially during the breeding season.

The Grey Wagtail always breeds near water, often building its nest in a crack or recess in a stone bridge above a stream. The young are fed on tiny aquatic insects caught by 'bobbing' on a rock in the water.

IDENTIFICATION

A long, slender, graceful wagtail, with mainly grey and black upperparts and bright yellow underparts. Male has black throat, bordered with white stripes around eye. Female has pale throat. In winter, Grey Wagtails lose most of the yellow from their plumage, except under the tail, but always appear more graceful and longer-tailed than Pied Wagtail. Beware confusion in spring and summer months with its close relative the Yellow Wagtail, which has greenish-olive upperparts, yellow head and underparts, and a shorter tail. Call a loud, 'tsee-sit', less harsh and strident than Pied.

IN THE GARDEN

STATUS AND HABITAT: In spring and summer, mainly a bird of upland regions, where it nests alongside fast-flowing water. In autumn and winter heads towards lowland areas, though always stays beside or near water. Found in gardens close to suitable habitat, although scarce or absent from parts of eastern England.

BREEDING: Breeds from March to August, making a cup-shaped nest in a crack under a bridge. Lays 4–6 eggs, buff with brown spots, and incubates for 11–14 days. Young fledge after two weeks. Often two, sometimes three, broods.

FEEDING: Feeds mainly on insects, though will occasionally take small fish and even amphibians.

Although often associated with fast-flowing streams in upland areas, the Grey Wagtail can be found in a variety of watery habitats, especially during the autumn and winter. Its steel-grey upperparts and yellow beneath the tail are distinctive.

PIED (WHITE) WAGTAIL

Motacilla alba Length 18 cm (7 in)

Our commonest and most familiar wagtail, found in urban and suburban areas throughout the country. Often feeds on open lawns, where its black-and-white plumage and wagging gait make it a popular garden visitor. British race darker than continental form, 'White Wagtail', which occasionally occurs here as a passage migrant in spring and autumn.

IDENTIFICATION

No other common garden bird has the Pied Wagtail's combination of long, wagging tail and black-and-white plumage. Male darker than female, with black crown, back, throat and upper breast; white underparts, cheeks, and two white wing-bars. Female has dark grey back, and less black on throat. Tail black with white outer feathers. In winter appears drabber and greyer. Continental race (White Wagtail) has paler back, contrasting strongly with black head and nape. Often seen in short, bouncing flight, where long tail and short wings are obvious. Call a loud, two-note 'chis-ikk'.

The male Pied Wagtail can be told apart from the female by its more contrasting black-and-white plumage. Both sexes of the Pied Wagtail are darker than the Continental race, known as the White Wagtail.

IN THE GARDEN

STATUS AND HABITAT: A common visitor, mainly feeding on open lawns, though often seen picking morsels from in between concrete paving slabs! Also perches on roofs. In winter, Pied Wagtails gather together in large, communal roosts, to keep warm during cold weather.
BREEDING: Breeds from April to August, nesting in cracks in walls or buildings. Lays 5–6 eggs, whitish with dark spots, and incubates for 11–16 days. Young fledge after 11–16 days. Usually two or three broods.
FEEDING: Feeds mainly on small invertebrates, usually picked off the ground.

The Pied Wagtail is a familiar garden visitor, often feeding on driveways and lawns, where it is often seen searching for tiny insects , while continuously wagging its long tail as it walks.

WAXWING

Bombycilla garrulus Length: 17–18 cm (6.5–7 in)

The Waxwing is one of our rarest and most beautiful garden visitors. It breeds in the spruce and pine forests of northern Scandinavia and Siberia, but occasionally flocks move south and west towards the British Isles in search of food. These 'irruptions' generally take place in late autumn, with the birds remaining here for the rest of the winter. Once Waxwings arrive in a garden, they will gorge themselves on berries, stripping the bushes bare before moving on.

IDENTIFICATION

In flight, a flock of Waxwings may momentarily resemble a group of Starlings. Once the birds have landed, however, the soft, pinkish-brown plumage, erect crest and red, yellow and black wing-pattern are unmistakable. The tail is black with a yellow band at the tip, and the rump grey. The species gets its name from the red, waxy tips to the wing, missing on young birds. Call a quiet trill, often uttered by several birds at once.

IN THE GARDEN

STATUS AND HABITAT: An irregular visitor – some years see thousands of birds, while in others there are hardly any. First arrivals usually in late October and November, the birds staying until March or even April, when they depart north to breed. Most are seen in eastern Britain, though in invasion years flocks can turn up almost anywhere.

The Waxwing is only an occasional autumn and winter visitor to Britain, when shortages of berries in its native Scandinavia force the birds to flee south and westwards in search of new food supplies. It is mainly seen in eastern areas.

Flocks of Waxwings often perch in prominent places, displaying their handsome pink plumage and prominent crest. This flock spent the winter in a Norfolk village, to the delight of local birdwatchers.

If you are lucky enough to have Waxwings visit your garden, be prepared for another invasion – by local birdwatchers anxious to see this splendid species!

FEEDING: In winter, Waxwings feed mainly on berries, being especially partial to red ones such as cotoneaster. However, during mild winter weather they can also be observed flycatching insects, their usual summer diet.

WREN

Troglodytes troglodytes Length: 9–10 cm (3.5–4 in)

Many people are astonished to discover that the Wren is our commonest breeding bird, with around ten million pairs in the British Isles. Despite this, its small size, fast flight and skulking habits make it hard to see well. Wrens normally give their presence away with a burst of loud and explosive song, or by their repetitive 'ticking' call, delivered from a prominent post or from deep inside a bush.

IDENTIFICATION

The Wren is one of our smallest birds, weighing only a few grams. Often seen in flight, where its tiny wings whirr rapidly to propel the stout body through the air. Once it lands, the cocked tail, plump body and delicately marked brown and grey plumage are diagnostic. Song a loud, explosive burst of notes, including rapid trills. Various calls, including a sharp 'chak' and a rattling churr.

IN THE GARDEN

STATUS AND HABITAT: Found in almost every garden, though owing to its small size and skulking habits it may be hard to see. Most prominent in winter, when hunger often makes it bolder, and in early spring, when males sing their extraordinary song. Wrens are often seen hopping unobtrusively around rockeries and the base of bushes and trees, in search of food.

BREEDING: Breeds from March

The Wren is currently our commonest breeding species, though like many small birds it is highly vulnerable to population crashes in harsh winters, when up to ninety per cent of the population may perish.

One of our smallest birds, the Wren's secretive and skulking habits can make it hard to see well. A close-up view reveals the subtlety of its plumage, together with its distinctive plump shape and cocked tail.

to July, building a domed nest in thick cover, usually close to the ground. Lays 5–8 whitish eggs, and incubates for 12–20 days. Young fledge after 2–3 weeks. Almost always double-brooded.

FEEDING: Mostly feeds on tiny invertebrates, which it finds amongst the soil and in crevices in trees.

DUNNOCK

Prunella modularis Length 14.5 cm (6 in)

One of our most common yet least familiar garden birds, often overlooked or mistaken for a sparrow as it searches for food on the ground or beneath thick foliage. The Dunnock was once more commonly known as the Hedge Sparrow, though it is in fact more closely related to thrushes and chats than to the familiar House Sparrow. Makes up for its dull appearance by its extraordinary breeding habits.

IDENTIFICATION

Superficially appears to be a dull, brown, sparrow-like bird. However, on a closer look the thin, warbler-like bill, rufous upperparts streaked with black, and purplish-grey face, throat and breast become apparent. Legs orangey-pink. Song a rapid,

One of our least conspicuous garden birds, the Dunnock is nevertheless a common resident in gardens throughout the region. It usually feeds on the ground, poking amongst the leaf-litter for insects or seeds.

wren-like warbling, on a limited series of notes, which starts and finishes abruptly.

IN THE GARDEN

STATUS AND HABITAT: A common resident in gardens large or small throughout the country, although its skulking habits sometimes make it hard to see well. Usually feeds on the ground, creeping around with a horizontal gait, picking up morsels of food.

BREEDING: Breeds from March to August, nesting in low, thick undergrowth such as brambles or other scrubby bushes. Lays 4–6 bright blue eggs, and incubates for 12–13 days. Young fledge after 11–12 days. Raises two or sometimes three broods. Has highly complex breeding habits, including multiple pairing and polygamy, so several males and females may be present together during the breeding season.

FEEDING: Feeds on small insects, though in winter will also take seeds. Also enjoys mealworms when provided by householders.

Once known as the Hedge Sparrow, the Dunnock is actually more closely related to thrushes, robins and chats, as can be seen from its thin, pointed bill. The word Dunnock literally means "brown bird".

ROBIN

Erithacus rubecula Length 14 cm (5.5 in)

The Robin must surely be the most familiar and popular garden bird of all, inevitably topping popularity polls amongst British birds. Its confiding nature and attractive plumage have endeared it to generations of gardeners, although in reality the Robin is an aggressive species, with males sometimes fighting to the death to defend their territory.

IDENTIFICATION

Adult unmistakable. Male and female basically identical, with brown crown, wings, upperparts and tail, a grey band along the sides of the breast, white belly and the famous 'red breast' – actually a deep orange colour. Juvenile birds can cause confusion, however, as they lack red in their plumage, being a rather dull, spotty brown in colour. Robins sing all year round, defending summer and winter territories with their fluty, melodic song. Also call frequently – a sharp, metallic 'tic, tic, tic'.

Unlike many other birds, Robins remain solitary during the autumn and winter, with both males and females holding winter territories. As a result, they sing throughout the winter months.

IN THE GARDEN

STATUS AND HABITAT: Found in almost every garden, the Robin is one of our tamest birds, happily feeding alongside humans as they work. Will often take live food such as earthworms or mealworms from the hand. In harsh winter weather Robins become even more confiding, as they are vulnerable to food shortages caused by snow and ice.

BREEDING: Breeds from March to August, building a cup-shaped nest from grass and leaves, lined with hair. Lays 4–6 pale bluish-white eggs, lightly spotted with red, and incubates for 13–15 days. Young fledge after 12–14 days. Often two broods. Highly territorial, with the resident male seeing off any intruders as soon as they appear.

FEEDING: Feeds mainly on insects, although will also take seeds and fruit in winter.

With its orange breast, perky manner and confiding habits, the Robin must surely be our most popular and familiar garden bird. Despite its endearing appearance, however, the Robin can be aggressive and pugnacious, especially when defending its breeding territory.

NIGHTINGALE

Luscinia megarhynchos Length 16.5 cm (6.5 in)

Europe's most famous songster, the Nightingale, has for centuries been justly celebrated by poets and naturalists for the purity and beauty of its song. Although Nightingales sing by day as well as by night, they are often very difficult to see, as they hide deep in the heart of a bush or tree. Like many birds with a beautiful song, the Nightingale's plumage is a dull brown and is rather unmemorable.

IDENTIFICATION

A bulky bird looking rather like a Robin, with deep brown upperparts, greyish-white underparts and a rufous tail, which it often holds cocked to the rest of the body. Nightingales are best identified by their extraordinary and far-carrying song, incorporating a wide variety of deep and rich tones, sounds and notes, which once heard can never be forgotten. Beware, however, songsters such as the Blackcap, Blackbird or Song Thrush, which can sometimes recall the sound of the Nightingale.

The extraordinary and beautiful song of the Nightingale is legendary, having long been celebrated in European culture. Delivered by day as well as by night, it is most commonly heard in early May, when the birds return from Africa to breed.

IN THE GARDEN

STATUS AND HABITAT: The Nightingale is mainly found in scrubby areas on the edge of mixed or deciduous woodland, and may be seen (or more often heard) in well-wooded, rural gardens in the south-east of England and in Europe. Summer visitor, returning in late April and early May, and leaving from July–October.

BREEDING: Breeds from late April to July, building its nest in thick cover such as brambles, usually near the ground. Lays 4–5 greyish, brownish or olive-coloured eggs, and incubates for 13–14 days. Young fledge after 11–12 days. One brood.

A shy and elusive species, the Nightingale can sometimes be glimpsed as it hunts for insects on the forest floor. A rather dull, brown bird, it can be identified by its shape and distinctively cocked tail.

FEEDING: Feeds on insects and other invertebrates, taken from the ground, usually under cover of trees or bushes.

BLACK REDSTART

Phoenicurus ochruros Length 14 cm (5.5 in)

Originally a bird of mainly mountainous regions, the Black Redstart has spread north throughout Europe, often nesting in urban habitats such as power stations and industrial estates. During the years following the Second World War, the species took full advantage of disused bomb-sites to colonize southern Britain. However, it remains a rare breeding bird in the British Isles, confined mainly to the south and east of the country.

IDENTIFICATION

Breeding male unmistakable: with sooty-black face, throat and breast shading to grey on the belly; grey cap and back; dark wings with pale wing-patch; and the rusty-red tail which gives the species its name. Female also has rusty tail, but rest of plumage sooty-brown, darker than Common Redstart. In winter, male more like female. Best located by song: several short, scratchy phrases, with sharp, metallic sound like the clash of ball-bearings. Often sings from high perch – on a rooftop or a tower.

IN THE GARDEN

STATUS AND HABITAT: May occasionally be seen in gardens in built-up areas, particularly those near industrial sites. On the Continent the species also regularly occurs in smaller towns and villages, especially in mountainous regions. In autumn and winter moves to coastal areas, where males may establish a winter territory.
BREEDING: Breeds from March to August, building cup of leaves or grass on ledges or cavities in buildings. Lays 4–6 white eggs, and incubates for

The Black Redstart, unlike its woodland relative the Common Redstart, is mainly a bird of mountainous country. However, in northern parts of its range it has adapted to live in urban and industrial settings.

12–17 days. Young fledge after 16–18 days. Two, sometimes three, broods.
FEEDING: Feeds on insects, sometimes caught by flycatching in the air.

As its name suggests, the Black Redstart is a mainly black bird with a reddish-orange tail. Males often sing their characteristic, metallic song from a prominent post, rock or rooftop.

BLACKBIRD

Turdus merula Length 24–25 cm (9–10 in)

With his deep, fluty song, the male Blackbird is arguably the champion songster of all our garden birds. A member of the thrush family, the Blackbird is widely distributed throughout the British Isles, and a regular visitor to urban, suburban and rural gardens. Blackbirds are also champion breeders, with one pair raising up to five broods in a single season!

With its black plumage, yellow bill and beady eye, the male Blackbird is one of our most familiar and best-loved garden birds. Its varied and musical song, delivered from high in a tree, is often the first sound of the dawn chorus.

IDENTIFICATION

The male Blackbird, as his name suggests, has an all-black plumage, apart from a bright yellow bill and pale ring around the eye. Females dark brown, with lighter streaking on the throat and breast. Beware of males with variable amounts of white in their plumage, as despite its name the Blackbird is prone to albinism. Song a rich, varied melody, delivered at a deliberate, slow pace, with frequent pauses between each phrase. Unlike the Song Thrush, the Blackbird rarely repeats phrases in its song.

IN THE GARDEN

STATUS AND HABITAT: The Blackbird is one of the earliest singers to begin the dawn chorus, and its song is perhaps the most familiar of all garden birds. Blackbirds defend territories from early in the year, and sometimes begin to build their nests when snow is still lying on the ground.

BREEDING: Breeds from March to August, building an untidy, cup-shaped nest lined with mud. Lays 3–5 eggs, pale greenish in colour spotted with brownish-red. Incubates for 12–15 days, and young fledge after a further 12–15 days. Blackbirds will raise up to five broods, the female often laying new clutches while the male is still feeding young from the previous brood.

FEEDING: In spring and summer, feeds mainly on insects and earthworms taken from the soil. In autumn and winter, adopts a more catholic diet, including fruit.

The female Blackbird has an all-brown plumage, making her far less conspicuous than her mate. A prolific breeder, Blackbirds may raise up to five broods in a single nesting season.

FIELDFARE

Turdus pilaris Length 25–26 cm (10 in)

The Fieldfare, along with its smaller relative the Redwing, is mainly a winter visitor to the British Isles from its native Scandinavia. The first Fieldfares arrive here in late autumn, often in huge flocks. However, if hard weather occurs on the continent later in the winter, we may see a second invasion, as the birds flee westwards in search of milder weather and new sources of food – which they often find in gardens.

IDENTIFICATION

Of all the European thrushes, the Fieldfare is second only to the Mistle Thrush in size, being not much smaller than a pigeon. Fieldfares are wary birds, often shy and unapproachable, although given close views they are very attractive. More colourful than other thrushes, with a steel-grey head, deep rufous back and wings, grey rump and black tail. Underparts are pale yellowish, strongly marked with thick black chevrons. Powerful, undulating flight. Call a harsh chattering 'chak-chak-chak'.

IN THE GARDEN

STATUS AND HABITAT: Winter visitor, usually arriving in late October or November, with some birds staying into March or even April. Gregarious, often forming mixed feeding flocks with other thrush species. The Fieldfare visits gardens far less regularly than the Redwing, and normally only when hard winter weather causes food shortages in the surrounding countryside.

FEEDING: During winter, feeds mainly on fruits and berries, greedily stripping bushes bare. May also be attracted to gardens by fruit placed on the ground, especially during snowy weather.

Large flocks of Fieldfares travel south and west from Scandinavia to spend the winter in the British Isles, where they occasionally visit gardens in the company of other thrushes such as the Redwing.

Berries are a favourite food of the Fieldfare. A flock of birds can strip a bush bare in a matter of hours, before moving on in search of new supplies elsewhere.

115

SONG THRUSH

Turdus philomelos Length 23 cm (9 in)

For many town and city-dwellers, the sight and sound of a Song Thrush sitting on a roof at sunset, heralds the end of winter and arrival of spring. Its repetitive, deliberate and tuneful song is one of the most popular of all our breeding birds' songs. Our most familiar thrush, it is a common visitor to many gardens, although in recent years has suffered a steep decline in numbers, for reasons we do not yet fully understand.

Above: *With its spotted breast, confiding habits and repetitive but tuneful song, the Song Thrush is one of our most familiar garden birds. However, in recent years it has undergone a rapid decline, and may be absent from its usual haunts.*

Right: *Song Thrushes frequently feed on lawns, where they pull up worms and other small invertebrates. They will also smash snails on a hard surface to expose the contents of the shell and eat them.*

IDENTIFICATION

A small, neat-looking thrush, distinguished from the larger Mistle Thrush by its size, darker brown plumage, and smaller, neater spots on the throat and breast. Head and upperparts plain chocolate-brown; underparts whitish (yellower on the breast), and entirely covered with small, neat spots. In flight, shows buffish underwing. Song very distinctive: fluty in tone, less deep than the Blackbird, and consisting of short, measured phrases, often repeated in groups of two or three.

IN THE GARDEN

STATUS AND HABITAT: Until its recent decline, one of the commonest garden birds throughout Britain. In winter, British Song Thrushes often migrate south to France and Spain, their place being taken by birds from the Low Countries.

BREEDING: Breeds from March to July, building a cup-shaped nest from grass and small twigs, lined with mud. Lays 3–5 eggs, pale sky-blue spotted with black. Incubates for 12–14 days, young fledging after 12–15 days. Often raises two or three broods.

FEEDING: Feeds on invertebrates, including earthworms and snails, which it smashes on a stone or rock (an 'anvil') before eating the contents.

REDWING

Turdus iliacus Length 21 cm (8 in)

Our smallest thrush, the Redwing is a regular, widespread winter visitor to most parts of the British Isles from its Scandinavian breeding-grounds. Its attractive appearance makes this charming thrush a welcome garden visitor during harsh winter weather, when a feeding flock can strip a bush bare of berries within a few hours. Often seen in the company of other thrushes, especially Fieldfares.

Right: *Redwings are very partial to rotting fruit, especially windfall apples. In hard winter weather these food supplies can make the difference between life and death for this delightful thrush.*

Below: *Like its larger cousin the Fieldfare, the Redwing is a common and familiar winter visitor to the British Isles, where it flies from its breeding-grounds in Scandinavia. Its small size, creamy eyestripe and the orange-red patch on the flanks distinguish it from all other thrushes.*

IDENTIFICATION

A small, neat, dark thrush, with a prominent creamy eye-stripe and the deep orange-red patch on the sides of the breast which gives the species its name. Crown and upperparts dark brown; underparts pale whitish in colour, heavily streaked with dark brown. In flight, reddish patch on flanks and underwing is obvious. Can be confused with the larger Song Thrush, but darker colour and differences of plumage distinctive. Flight call a thin, high 'tseeep'.

IN THE GARDEN

STATUS AND HABITAT: Winter visitor, first arriving in the British Isles in late October or November, and departing north to breed in March or April. Redwings often visit gardens, especially during harsh winter weather, when their smaller size makes them more vulnerable than their relatives. Will frequently take food provided by humans. Forms loose flocks of a dozen or more birds, often with other thrush species.

FEEDING: In winter, feeds mainly on fruit and berries.

MISTLE THRUSH

Turdus viscivorus Length 27 cm (10.5 in)

Our largest thrush, always appearing bulky and heavy whether in flight or on the ground. Mistle Thrushes are often heard before they are seen, giving their harsh, chattering call while flying overhead. Named after its fondness for Mistletoe berries, the species is known in many country areas as the Stormcock, owing to its habit of singing before thunderstorms, even continuing during heavy rain.

IDENTIFICATION

Large and bulky, told apart from Song Thrush by size, paler, greyer appearance, and heavier spotting on breast. Upperparts pale grey-brown, with paler edges to the wings. Underparts pale cream, with heavy black spotting, merging into dark smudges on throat and breast. Large, heavy bill. When flying can appear pigeon-like, though flight undulating rather than direct. Tail-feathers have white edges – often visible in flight. Harsh, rattling call. Song cross between Blackbird and Song Thrush: deep and fluty but with regular repetitions of phrase.

The Mistle Thrush can be told apart from its smaller relative the Song Thrush by its larger size, pale plumage and heavy spotting on the underparts. When flushed it flies off, giving a harsh, rattling call.

Mistle Thrushes are shy birds, but visit gardens, especially those with large, mature trees and wide, open areas of lawn. In summer they feed mainly on invertebrates, though in winter they will also take berries and fruit.

IN THE GARDEN

STATUS AND HABITAT: A familiar visitor to gardens all over the country, especially those with large, mature trees. Some British Mistle Thrushes migrate to southern Europe for the winter, with continental immigrants taking their place.

BREEDING: Breeds from March to July, building a large, cup-shaped nest, often in the fork of a tree. Lays 3–5 large eggs, bluish-green speckled with brown. Incubates for 12–15 days, and young fledge after a further 12–16 days. Often two broods.

FEEDING: Feeds on invertebrates, mainly taken from the ground. Like other thrushes, will also take fruit and berries in winter.

WHITETHROAT

Sylvia communis Length 14 cm (5.5 in)

Once a common and familiar summer visitor to Britain and Europe, the Whitethroat suffered a major population crash during the late 1960s and 1970s. This was due to a severe drought in the species' winter-quarters, the Sahel Zone in western Africa. Since then, the Whitethroat has made a partial recovery, though it remains very vulnerable to climate change.

IDENTIFICATION

A large, colourful, long-winged warbler, sporting the white throat which gives the species its name. Male has greyish-brown head, brown back, peachy-white underparts and dark brown wings with a rufous wing-patch. Female duller, though also shows pale throat and rufous on wings. Tail dark with pale outer feathers. Song a pleasant, chattering warble, brief but soon repeated.

IN THE GARDEN

STATUS AND HABITAT: The Whitethroat is mainly a bird of hedgerows, scrub and other open areas, so is not naturally a garden bird. However, as one of our

The male Whitethroat is one of our most handsome and attractive warblers, with a grey head, rufous wings, and distinctive white throat which gives the species its name. After a decline due to drought in its African wintering quarters, the species now appears to be making a recovery.

common, regular migrants it can and does turn up in gardens, especially during spring or autumn.

BREEDING: Breeds from April to July, nesting low in thick bushes. Lays 4–5 pale eggs with dark spots, and incubates for 11–14 days. Young fledge after 10–12 days. One, often two, broods.

FEEDING: Feeds on insects during breeding season, but in late summer and autumn feeds on berries, to build up energy in preparation for the long journey south to Africa.

The female Whitethroat resembles a duller version of the male. Whitethroats generally breed in areas of open scrub, building a tidy, cup-shaped nest in brambles or other thick cover.

119

GARDEN WARBLER

Sylvia borin Length 14 cm (5.5 in)

Despite its name, this species is not a common visitor to gardens, instead preferring mixed woodland and scrub. The Garden Warbler's unmarked plumage and skulking habits make it a difficult bird to see, let alone identify. Best detected by its unobtrusive but attractive song, which recalls its close relative the Blackcap, but is less tuneful and faster in pace.

IN THE GARDEN

STATUS AND HABITAT: Summer visitor, not usually arriving until early to mid-May, and departing in August. Prefers to nest in thick, dense undergrowth with a fairly open tree canopy, such as small hawthorn copses. Therefore rare except in larger gardens in rural areas.

BREEDING: Breeds from May to July, building a nest in thick, low cover. Lays 4–5 eggs, pale with light spotting. Incubates for 10–12 days, and young fledge after 9–12 days. Sometimes double-brooded.

FEEDING: Feeds mainly on insects, which it finds in dense foliage.

Left: *Like many warblers, the Garden Warbler builds a nest from dry grass stems, lined with grass and hair, usually found low in thick cover. The young fledge very quickly, as little as nine days after hatching.*

Below: *A shy and unobtrusive bird, the best indication that the Garden Warbler is present is its distinctive song, a rapid warbling recalling a speeded-up Blackcap. It is a summer visitor to Britain, generally arriving in early May.*

IDENTIFICATION

A large, bulky warbler, almost entirely devoid of identification features! Appears pale brownish-grey, and unstreaked, with 'open' face-pattern and dark, beady eye. At close range, upperparts appear slightly darker, especially on wingtips. Underparts pale buff. Legs grey. Beware confusion with brownish Chiffchaffs – especially in autumn – although they are much smaller and usually show traces of green in the plumage. Song a quiet, gentle, warbling, similar to Blackcap but lacking range and fluty notes.

BLACKCAP

Sylvia atricapilla Length 14 cm (5.5 in)

One of our commonest and most widespread summer visitors, its early arrival and deep, fluty song once earned it the folk-name of 'March Nightingale'. In recent years, birds from central Europe have changed their migratory habits, and headed north and west to spend the winter in Britain, becoming familiar visitors to garden bird-tables. Only the male has the black cap which gives the species its name.

IDENTIFICATION

A large warbler, with a mainly grey plumage. Males possess the distinctive black cap; females have a chestnut brown cap instead. Wings slightly darker than rest of upperparts; underparts paler. Legs dark. In the breeding season, best discovered by its song, which combines a warbler-like variety with the fluty tones of the Blackbird.

IN THE GARDEN

STATUS AND HABITAT: In the breeding season, prefers fairly dense scrub, with tall bushes or trees. Occasional visitor to gardens, mainly those near mixed, scrubby woodland. Blackcaps are far more likely to visit your garden during the winter, especially during a spell of snow and ice, when they can be found feeding on bird tables or from windfall apples on the lawn. Winter birds arrive from late autumn, reaching their peak in December to February.

BREEDING: Summer visitors return early, from late March or April, and stay until August or September. Breeds from April to August, nesting in low, thick cover. Lays 4–6 eggs, pale with fine spots, and incubates for 10–12 days. Young fledge after 10–13 days. Sometimes two broods.

FEEDING: In spring and summer, feeds on insects. During autumn and winter changes diet to mainly fruit, often provided directly or indirectly by people.

The male Blackcap sports the black crown which gives the species its name. A large, bulky warbler, it is one of our commonest summer visitors, often located by its attractive, fluty song.

Females have a brown, rather than black, crown. Birds from central Europe now spend the winter in Britain, often visiting gardens in search of food.

CHIFFCHAFF

Phylloscopus collybita Length 11 cm (4–4.5 in)

The monotonous but cheering two-note song which gives the Chiffchaff its name is one of the first signs that spring is returning to the British Isles. One of the earliest migrants to return, with the first arrivals in March, in recent years Chiffchaffs have also begun to overwinter here in increasing numbers, often visiting gardens, especially in the south and west.

IDENTIFICATION

A small, leaf-coloured warbler, superficially indistinguishable from its close relative the Willow Warbler, though easily told apart by their respective songs. Generally duller, browner and less yellowish than Willow Warbler, with dark legs and feet. Upperparts greenish-grey, with darker edges to wing-feathers; underparts whitish-buff; short, pale stripe just above eye. Unique song – unlike any other warbler, repeating a combination of two syllables: 'chiff-chaff-chiff-chiff-chaff'.

The Chiffchaff is, at first sight, very similar to its close relative the Willow Warbler. The two species are best told apart by sound, with the Chiffchaff's rather monotonous song in great contrast to the Willow Warbler's more musical offering.

IN THE GARDEN

STATUS AND HABITAT: Summer migrants return as early as mid-March, and stay until August or September. However, Chiffchaffs now also winter in Britain in small numbers, especially in the milder south and west of the country.

BREEDING: Breeds from April to August, nesting on or near the ground in thick undergrowth. Lays 4–7 eggs, white with a few dark spots, and incubates for 13–15 days. Young fledge after 12–15 days. One, sometimes two, broods.

FEEDING: Feeds on insects, usually gleaned high in the canopy of trees or bushes. May also take some fruit in autumn and winter, and has been observed feeding on peanuts.

The Chiffchaff builds a domed nest out of grasses, moss and dead leaves, lined with feathers. Unlike the Willow Warbler, Chiffchaffs usually build their nest a little above the ground, often in thick foliage.

WILLOW WARBLER

Phylloscopus trochilus Length 11.5 cm (4.5 in)

By far our commonest summer visitor, found all over northern Europe. Several million pairs breed each year in the British Isles. Despite this, because of its rather dull appearance and unobtrusive habits this bird is hardly known except by birdwatchers. Once heard, however, the Willow Warbler's poignant song, an arpeggio of silvery notes descending the scale, can never be forgotten.

IDENTIFICATION

A small, yellowish-green warbler, distinguished from its relative the Chiffchaff by pale legs, yellower plumage and more prominent stripe above the eye - though the difference in song is easily the best way to tell the two species apart. Upperparts olive-green, darker on edges to wing-feathers; underparts pale yellowish-green. Autumn juveniles appear bright yellow underneath. Song a delicious sequence of bright, silvery notes, running down the scale and gathering speed at the end. Beware similar rhythm of Chaffinch, which has a much more powerful and harsher song.

IN THE GARDEN

STATUS AND HABITAT: Summer visitor, returning from mid-April and departing in August–September. Sometimes found in gardens, especially in rural areas near suitable habitat. Family parties may also be seen in late summer, after dispersing from the nest.

BREEDING: Breeds from May to August, nesting in base of thick foliage on the ground. Lays 4–8 eggs, white with light speckling, and incubates for 12–14 days. Young fledge after 11–15 days. One, occasionally two, broods.

FEEDING: Feeds on insects, obtained by flycatching or by gleaning from branches of a tree.

Despite being the commonest summer visitor to northern Europe, the Willow Warbler is more often heard than seen. Its song is a silvery cascade of notes descending the scale, with a rather melancholy and wistful tone.

Willow Warblers build their nest on the ground, concealed by thick foliage to avoid predators. The young are often seen in late summer, foraging for food together with their parents.

GOLDCREST

Regulus regulus Length 9 cm (3.5 in)

Europe's smallest bird (along with its cousin the Firecrest), weighing a mere five grams – just one-fifth of an ounce. A minute, jewel-like sprite, the Goldcrest is often seen flitting from leaf to leaf while uttering a call almost too high to be audible to the human ear. Despite its tiny size, it manages to stay resident in northern Europe through even the harshest winters, finding food and shelter deep within the region's great coniferous forests.

IDENTIFICATION

Tiny, plump, with a mainly greenish plumage. Upperparts yellowish-green, with dark edges to wing feathers and two pale wingbars. Underparts pale greyish-white. Head-pattern gives the species its name: broad gold stripe along crown, bordered on either side by black. Beady eye. Juvenile lacks crown-stripe. Song a high, thin warble; call a high-pitched, three-note 'see-see-see'.

IN THE GARDEN

STATUS AND HABITAT: Found in small numbers in suburban and rural areas throughout the country, though small size and skulking habits sometimes make it hard to detect. Prefers conifers, often breeding in large coniferous forests. More common in gardens during the winter months.

BREEDING: Breeds from March to August, nesting almost exclusively in conifers, where it builds a tiny nest hanging from the end of a branch. Lays 7–12 minuscule eggs, white with fine spots, and incubates for 16 days. Young fledge after 19 days. Two broods.

FEEDING: Feeds on tiny insects, gleaned from twigs and foliage.

The Goldcrest uses its sharp claws to cling upside-down on twigs and leaves, enabling it to feed on tiny insects and spiders. Both male and female have the distinctive gold crown which gives the species its name.

The Goldcrest builds its nest on the very tips of twigs, using spiders' webs to bind together a basket of moss, which it lines with tiny feathers. The chicks are fed on insects gleaned from nearby foliage.

FIRECREST

Regulus ignicapillus Length 9 cm (3.5 in)

The Firecrest shares with its commoner relative, the Goldcrest, the distinction of being Europe's smallest and lightest species of bird. A jewel of a bird, with its delicately marked plumage and fiery orange crown, which gives the species its name. Firecrests are difficult to find, and are often overlooked because of their similarity to their commoner cousin.

Above: *Along with its close relative the Goldcrest, the Firecrest is Europe's smallest breeding bird. They can be told apart by the Firecrest's distinctive black and cream head-pattern, bronze shoulder-patch and deep orange crown.*

Right: *The Firecrest breeds in a wide variety of woodland habitats, where it is most likely to be located by its distinctive song: like a plainer version of the Goldcrest's.*

IDENTIFICATION

Brighter and more colourful than the Goldcrest, from which it is told apart by the distinctive black-and-white head-pattern, deeper orange crown (male only), and bronze patch on shoulders. Female similar to male, but with yellow crown. Song high-pitched like Goldcrest's but plainer and briefer, a series of rapid 'zits' with no real variation. Call like Goldcrest's but deeper and harsher.

IN THE GARDEN

STATUS AND HABITAT: The Firecrest is less partial to coniferous woodlands than the Goldcrest, although it can occur in any suitable wooded habitat. A very rare and localized breeder in southern Britain, but fairly common throughout continental Europe. In autumn and winter the northern populations move to the coastal areas.

BREEDING: Breeds from April to August, in coniferous or deciduous woodland, building a hanging nest from the ends of a branch. Lays 7–12 whitish eggs, and incubates for 14–16 days. Young fledge after 19–24 days. Two broods.

FEEDING: Feeds mainly on insects, gleaned from twigs and leaves. May take larger prey than Goldcrest.

SPOTTED FLYCATCHER

Muscicapa striata Length 14 cm (5.5 in)

One of the latest summer visitors to return, Spotted Flycatchers sometimes don't arrive back in the British Isles until late May. Once here, this charming but unobtrusive bird lives up to its name by leaping into the air on long, slender wings to catch flying insects. In recent years the Spotted Flycatcher has undergone a major decline, probably owing to drought in sub-Saharan Africa.

IDENTIFICATION

A slim, attractive bird, best identified by its flycatching habits. Generally greyish-brown, with unmarked brown upperparts, a pale wingbar, and pale buff underparts with light brown streaks on the breast. Head-shape distinctive, with slightly raised

Juvenile Spotted Flycatchers are neater than their parents, and show the same rather dull brown plumage, beady black eye and upright posture. They soon learn to feed by flycatching.

crest, long thin bill, and beady black eye. Crown slightly streaked. Legs dark. Song a rather unmemorable sequence of thin squeaks.

IN THE GARDEN

STATUS AND HABITAT: Summer visitor, returning in May and departing in August–September. Often nests in large gardens, especially those in rural areas, which offer suitable nesting sites, such as old walls.

BREEDING: Breeds from May to August, nesting in holes or crevices. Lays 4–6 eggs, varying from buff to greenish-blue, with reddish blotches. Incubates for 12–14 days, and young fledge after 12–16 days. Sometimes raises two broods, especially in warm, dry summers.

FEEDING: Feeds almost exclusively on flying insects caught in mid-air, though in bad weather will also feed from ground.

The Spotted Flycatcher, as its name suggests, feeds mainly on small insects caught in flight. Typically, the bird sits on a suitable perch before launching itself into mid-air to seize its prey.

LONG-TAILED TIT

Aegithalos caudatus Length 12–14 cm (5–5.5 in)

A sudden flurry of activity, accompanied by high-pitched twittering, signals the arrival of a foraging flock of Long-tailed Tits. Bouncing from twig to twig like balls of fluff, they can be amazingly approachable, before springing away to find food elsewhere. Long-tailed Tits build an extraordinary, ball-shaped nest, which gives the species the folk-name 'bumbarrel'.

IDENTIFICATION

No other bird has such a long tail in proportion to its body. This, combined with fluffy black, cream and pink plumage, make the Long-tailed Tit easy to identify. Upperparts mainly dark black, with streaks of pink and white on the back and wings. Underparts white, tinged pink on the belly. A thick black stripe runs from the base of the bill, above the eye, to the nape. Crown whitish. Tail black with white edges. Often heard just before seen: a variety of high-pitched calls, including clicks, whistles and a piercing, trisyllabic 'tseee-tseee-tseee', to keep contact with the flock.

With its pink, black and cream plumage, together with a plump body and long tail, the Long-tailed Tit is unmistakable. Long-tailed Tits usually travel in flocks, giving away their presence by their high-pitched calls.

IN THE GARDEN

STATUS AND HABITAT: Long-tailed Tits spend the winter in flocks of a dozen or more, constantly searching for food in an agile and acrobatic fashion. They rarely stay long in one spot, appearing and disappearing in a few seconds. In spring and summer they pair off to breed, although after breeding are often seen in family parties.

BREEDING: Breeds from March to July, building a ball-shaped nest from feathers, held together with spiders' webs and well camouflaged with lichens. Lays 7–12 tiny eggs, white with a few spots, and incubates for 13–17 days. Young fledge after 15–16 days. One brood, but adults often 'help' at the nest of a relative.

FEEDING: Feeds on insects, especially a variety of tiny larvae and spiders.

Long-tailed Tits build an extraordinary, ball-shaped nest out of moss, hair and cobwebs, covered with lichen and lined with tiny feathers. The entrance hole is usually at or near the top.

MARSH TIT

Parus palustris Length 11.5 cm (4.5 in)

Despite its name, the Marsh Tit is not particularly fond of damp places, and can be found in a wide variety of woodland habitats throughout England and Wales. It can be very hard to tell apart from its close relative the Willow Tit; indeed the two were thought to be the same species until early this century.

IDENTIFICATION

A small, plump, brownish-grey tit with a distinctive black cap and bib, and white cheeks. Upperparts mid greyish-brown, lacking the white wing-panel of Willow Tit. Underparts paler, greyish-buff. Black cap glossy, rather than matt, extending just below eye. Head smaller than Willow Tit. Best told apart by call: a sharp 'pit-chu', or a whistled 'chu-chu-chu'.

IN THE GARDEN

STATUS AND HABITAT: A not uncommon visitor to many gardens, especially those in rural areas near extensive woodland. Fairly shy, but will sometimes visit bird-tables and nut-feeders in winter. Beware confusion with the larger, slimmer, greyer Blackcap, whose cap ends just above the eye, rather than below. Not found in Ireland or Scotland.

BREEDING: Breeds from April to July, usually nesting in a natural hole in rotten wood. Lays 7–11 eggs, white with a few spots, and incubates for 13–15 days. Young fledge after 17–21 days. One brood.

FEEDING: Feeds on invertebrates in spring and summer, and seeds and berries during autumn and winter. Will also feed on peanuts.

Above: *Like its close relative the Willow Tit, the Marsh Tit has a distinctive black cap and white cheeks. The two are best told apart by the Marsh Tit's glossy cap, slimmer build and the difference in their songs.*

Left: *Marsh Tits are usually found in areas of mixed woodland, though they will often visit bird tables along with other species of tit, especially during the autumn and winter.*

128

WILLOW TIT

Parus montanus Length 11.5 cm (4.5 in)

The Willow Tit was discovered as a British bird only at the turn of the century, and is still one of our least well-known breeding species. The Willow Tit has recently undergone a sharp decline in numbers, and today is absent from many of its former haunts. May sometimes be overlooked due to the similarity to its commoner relative, the Marsh Tit.

IDENTIFICATION

Easily confused with Marsh Tit, although given good views can be quite distinctive. Usually looks bulkier, owing to its larger head and thick, bull-like neck. Also appears more colourful than Marsh Tit, with a pale panel on the wings and a tinge of russet along the flanks. Black bib usually larger than the Marsh Tit's, and black cap is matt rather than glossy, though this can be difficult to see except in very good light. Distinctive call: a harsh, nasal 'chay-chay-chay'.

IN THE GARDEN

STATUS AND HABITAT: Like the Marsh Tit, this bird is mainly confined to England and Wales, where it has

A fairly uncommon visitor to gardens, the Willow Tit has recently undergone a serious decline in numbers and range, possibly due to loss of its preferred damp, wooded habitats.

Less common than the Marsh Tit, which it closely resembles. Best told apart by more bull-necked posture, sooty cap and pale panel on the wing, giving it a brighter appearance.

a patchy distribution, being absent from many apparently suitable habitats. A rare visitor to gardens, Willow Tits may sometimes be found near damp habitats, especially where alders grow. These birds are not found in Ireland.

BREEDING: Breeds from April to July, excavating a nest-hole in a rotting tree-stump. Lays 6–9 eggs, white with a few spots, and incubates for 13–15 days. Young fledge after 17–20 days. One brood.

FEEDING: Feeds on insects all year round, but like the Marsh Tit will broaden its diet in winter to include seeds and berries.

COAL TIT

Parus ater Length 11.5 cm (4.5 in)

During the breeding season, the Coal Tit shows a marked preference for coniferous woods and forests, although in autumn and winter they usually join other tit species, to search for food. With its acrobatic habits, the Coal Tit is one of our most welcome garden visitors, often visiting nut-feeders. Despite their tiny size, they are less affected by harsh winter weather than other small birds, probably because they are able to feed on the underside of snow-covered branches, and hoard food.

Above: *In autumn and winter, Coal Tits often join together with other small birds to form feeding flocks. They readily take to artificial food sources such as peanuts.*

Right: *The distinctive white patch on the Coal Tit's nape, together with its coal-black and warm brown plumage, tell it apart from other species of tit. This bird is a frequent visitor to gardens, especially those with or near conifers.*

IDENTIFICATION

At first sight the Coal Tit appears rather dull compared with Blue and Great Tits. However, on a closer inspection, its delicate plumage, combining black, white, brown and grey, becomes apparent. Like the Great Tit, it has white cheeks and a black cap and throat, but also sports a distinctive white patch on the nape. Upperparts grey, with two white wingbars. Underparts a delicate shade of buff. A variety of thin, high-pitched calls, rather like Goldcrest. Song rhythmic and repetitive, like weaker version of Great Tit's.

IN THE GARDEN

STATUS AND HABITAT: The Coal Tit is a regular winter visitor to many gardens, especially in parts of Scotland. Often appears in mixed groups of Blue and Great Tits, taking full advantage of any food on offer. Coal Tits are more likely to appear in gardens with conifers, or near a coniferous wood.

BREEDING: Breeds from April to July, usually nesting in a rotten stump near the ground. Lays 8–9 eggs, white with a few spots, and incubates for 13–18 days. Young fledge after 16–22 days. One brood.

FEEDING: Feeds mainly on insects and spiders, usually taken from pine needles. In autumn and winter will also take nuts from artificial feeders.

BLUE TIT

Parus caeruleus Length 11.5 cm (4.5 in)

One of the most familiar and best-loved of all British birds, the Blue Tit is a regular visitor to gardens throughout the year, delighting people everywhere with its acrobatic antics. As well as taking peanuts from feeders, Blue Tits have also learned to peck holes in the tops of milk-bottles to get at the contents. The species readily breeds in nestboxes, and young Blue Tits are a familiar sight throughout late spring and summer.

IDENTIFICATION

Our commonest tit, easily identified by its small size and blue-and-yellow plumage. In fact, the blue is confined to the crown, wings and tail, with the rest of the upperparts a dull green colour. Underparts are bright lemon-yellow, with an indistinct dark stripe bisecting the lower breast and belly. Head pattern shows whitish cheeks surrounded by a thin navy stripe running through the eyes. Like other tits, gives a wide variety of chattering calls, as well as a clear, ringing song 'pseet–see–sirrrrr'.

IN THE GARDEN

STATUS AND HABITAT: There can hardly be a garden in the United Kingdom, from the city centre to the heart of the countryside, that does not enjoy at least an occasional visit from Blue Tits. They travel in loose flocks in winter, and several individuals will compete to feed on bags of nuts or seeds. In spring and summer Blue Tits often nest in gardens, and are especially likely to utilize nestboxes.

BREEDING: Breeds from April to August, either using a natural cavity or artificial nestbox, in which it builds a loose nest from grass, feathers and moss. Lays 7–16 eggs, white with a few spots, and incubates for 13–16 days. Young fledge after 16–22 days. One brood.

FEEDING: Feeds on insects and spiders; in winter will readily feed on seeds and nuts provided by people.

Above: *Blue Tits usually nest in holes, cracks or cavities in trees, building a cup of moss and grass, which they line with hair and wool. They have a single brood, raising up to sixteen chicks.*

Left: *Our commonest species of tit, the Blue Tit is one of the most popular and familiar garden birds. It readily feeds on peanuts from artificial feeders, and is well-known for its tendency to break open foil milk-bottle tops to get at the cream inside.*

GREAT TIT

Parus major Length: 13.5–14.5 cm (5.5–6 in)

The Great Tit is one of our most familiar garden birds, found throughout Britain and western Europe. It is seen most often in winter, when it is a regular visitor to bird-tables and feeders. Great Tits often breed in nestboxes as well as natural nest-holes. Their repetitive, two-note song is one of the most familiar sounds of spring and early summer.

IDENTIFICATION

Given good views, the Great Tit is easily told apart from its smaller cousin the Blue Tit. Striking features include the black head, contrasting white cheeks, and the bright yellow breast, bisected by a thick black line. Upperparts mainly olive-green, shading to blue on the wings and tail, with a white wingbar. Young birds duller, with yellow cheeks. Great Tits have a bewildering variety of calls, the best-known being the repetitive two-note 'tea-cher, tea-cher', with the stress on the second syllable.

IN THE GARDEN

STATUS AND HABITAT: Great Tits can be found in the garden all year round, although numbers tend to

The Great Tit is a common and familiar garden visitor, easily identified by its black-and-yellow plumage and contrasting white cheeks. An aggressive bird, it will often dominate its smaller cousins at bird feeders and tables.

increase in late summer and autumn as newly fledged broods search for food. Predation and other natural mortality soon reduce numbers, though these are swelled in winter as birds from rural areas come into gardens in search of food.

BREEDING: Breeds March to July. Lays 5–11 eggs, white with reddish spots, and incubates for 11–15 days. Young fledge after about 3 weeks. One, occasionally two, broods. Frequently uses artificial nestboxes.

FEEDING: The Great Tit is an adaptable feeder. In winter, it prefers peanuts and seeds, and is adept at plundering feeding-stations. During the breeding-season, both adults and young feed on insects, especially caterpillars.

Originally a woodland species, the Great Tit has readily adapted to life in gardens, often breeding in artificial nestboxes. Its presence is given away by its distinctive two-note call.

NUTHATCH

Sitta europaea Length 14 cm (5.5 in)

Birds of the nuthatch family share a unique skill: they can climb vertically up or down a tree trunk or branch, using their powerful claws. A handsome bird, the Nuthatch is a welcome visitor to garden bird-tables, where it often fights off other species competing for food. Nuthatches are also known for hoarding food, storing nuts and seeds for future use.

or surrounded by woodland, especially during hard weather, when it will compete with tits and finches for food on peanut feeders. Very rare in Scotland and absent from Ireland. Nuthatches are highly territorial and mainly sedentary.

BREEDING: Breeds from March to July, nesting in natural holes in trees. Lays 6–8 eggs, white with a few reddish spots, and incubates for 13–18 days. Young fledge after 23–24 days. One brood.

FEEDING: Feeds on insects, although in winter will also take seeds and nuts. Often hoards food in preparation for hard weather.

Left: *With its blue-grey upperparts, orange-brown underparts, and black 'highwayman's mask' through the eye, the Nuthatch is a handsome and distinctive bird. It regularly visits rural gardens, especially during hard winter weather.*

Below: *With its strong, powerful claws, the Nuthatch is the only British species which can walk down, as well as up, tree-trunks. As its name suggests, it will often store nuts in crevices, to consume during food shortages.*

IDENTIFICATION

With its plump, pot-bellied shape, large, powerful beak and distinctive plumage, the Nuthatch is easy to identify, given good views. Crown, tail and upperparts steel-blue, darker on wings. Underparts rusty-orange, shading to deep orange beneath tail; white throat and cheeks; black stripe through eye. Short legs and large, powerful feet. Scandinavian birds much paler underneath. Song loud and penetrating: a repetitive 'piuu... piuu... piuu...'.

IN THE GARDEN

STATUS AND HABITAT: A regular visitor to gardens with mature trees

TREECREEPER

Certhia familiaris Length 12.5 cm (5 in)

More like a small rodent than a bird, the Treecreeper lives up to its name by creeping around the trunks and branches of trees, in search of tiny insects hidden beneath the bark. Treecreepers are one of the most sedentary of birds, and are highly vulnerable to prolonged spells of icy winter weather, especially when 'glazed frosts' cover twigs and branches with a thin layer of ice.

The Treecreeper uses its sharp claws to cling to the trunks and branches of trees, probing beneath the surface of the bark in search of tiny insects and spiders. The dull brown plumage and creeping habits mean that it is often hard to see.

IDENTIFICATION

Once seen well, unmistakable. A tiny, mouse-like bird, which seems to hug the side of a tree as it moves up and around in short, rapid jerks. Upperparts basically brown, though at close range the subtle streaks of white, yellow, buff and sepia making up the feather-pattern can be seen. Underparts white; tail rufous-brown. Bill long, slender and decurved. Rarely flies more than the distance to the next tree. Thin, high-pitched, piercing call; song Wren-like, with a rapid series of notes ending in a high trill.

IN THE GARDEN

STATUS AND HABITAT: A less frequent garden visitor than the Nuthatch, most likely to be seen in large, wooded gardens, or during hard winter weather. Found in suitable habitats throughout Britain and Ireland, apart from the extreme north and west. In winter joins mixed flocks of tits and Goldcrests in search of food.

BREEDING: Breeds from March to June, nesting in tiny cracks behind bark of tree, and occasionally using specially designed nestboxes. Lays 5–6 eggs, white with brownish spots, and incubates for 13–15 days. Young fledge after 14–16 days. One, sometimes two, broods.

FEEDING: Feeds on tiny insects and spiders taken from beneath the bark of trees.

Treecreepers build their nest in tiny cracks or crevices beneath the bark of a tree, using twigs, stems, roots, and bark. The nest is often concealed behind a curtain of ivy. In winter, Treecreepers often join mixed flocks of tits in search of food.

GOLDEN ORIOLE

Oriolus oriolus Length 24 cm (9.5 in)

Despite the bright black-and-yellow plumage of the male, the Golden Oriole is a shy and elusive bird, more often heard than seen. Once only a rare spring migrant to the British Isles, in recent years it has colonized parts of southern and eastern England, where it breeds in plantations of poplars. It is widespread throughout continental Europe north to southern Scandinavia, in parks, gardens and woodlands.

IDENTIFICATION

If seen well, male unmistakable, with bright golden-yellow plumage, black wings and red bill. Female much duller, with greenish-yellow head and back, yellow rump and tail-patches, and pale underparts with fine black streaks. Undulating, woodpecker-like flight, and indeed the female can sometimes be mistaken for a Green Woodpecker, but is much smaller. Song a haunting, melancholy, four-note whistle, rather thrush-like in character.

With his striking yellow and black plumage and bright red bill, the male Golden Oriole is one of Europe's most stunningly beautiful birds. Despite this, orioles can be very hard to see, as they spend most of the time hidden in dense foliage, high in the tree canopy.

Female Golden Orioles may superficially be mistaken for Green Woodpeckers, especially in flight. Orioles breed at the very tops of trees, suspending their nest from the outermost branches.

IN THE GARDEN

STATUS AND HABITAT: In Britain and Scandinavia, virtually confined as a breeding bird to poplars and alders, but farther south in Europe the oriole can be found in a much wider range of habitats, including parks and large, wooded gardens. Summer visitor, arriving late April to mid-May.

BREEDING: Breeds from May to July, building a suspended nest on outermost branches of a tree. Lays 2–5 eggs, white with dark blotches, and incubates for 14–18 days. Young fledge after 13–20 days, and breeding success is highly dependent on weather. One brood.

FEEDING: Feeds on insects, especially large caterpillars. Outside the breeding season will also take berries and fruit.

JAY

Garrulus glandarius Length 34 cm (13 in)

One of the handsomest of all our garden birds, the Jay belies the beauty of its plumage with its piratical and predatory habits, often raiding songbird nests for eggs and young. Usually shy and retiring, Jays may occasionally become surprisingly confiding in the presence of humans. The Jay population is boosted in autumn and winter by the arrival of immigrants from the continent.

IDENTIFICATION

A large, brightly coloured bird, with several distinctive plumage features. These include overall pinkish-brown plumage, a blue patch on the wing, and in flight, a bright, white rump. Crown lightly streaked, and sometimes raised as a crest; black 'moustache' and pale throat. Wings and tail black, with blue-and-white patches showing well in flight. Often calls: a harsh croak.

IN THE GARDEN

STATUS AND HABITAT: Despite its large size, the Jay can be shy and inconspicuous, especially during the breeding season. A woodland species, found in any garden with enough trees and bushes to provide cover. Absent from northern Scotland; generally scarce in Ireland.

BREEDING: Breeds from April to July, building its nest in the fork of a bush or tree. Lays 5–8 eggs, pale olive with fine speckling, and incubates for 16–17 days. Young fledge after 19–23 days. One brood.

FEEDING: Feeds on a wide variety of foods, although its staple diet is acorns, which it often hoards for future use. In spring and summer will take insects, eggs and the young of smaller birds.

Above: *The Jay's pinkish plumage, blue on the wing and short crest make it a handsome and distinctive bird. A member of the crow family, it shares its relatives' intelligence and predatory habits.*

Left: *Jays often visit gardens in winter, in search of food to supplement their staple diet of acorns. They are particularly partial to peanuts and mealworms, although will take a wide variety of foods.*

MAGPIE

Pica pica Length 44–48 cm (17–19 in)

Pied beauty or murderous villain? More than any other garden bird, the Magpie inspires affection and hatred in almost equal measure. But before we condemn Magpies for raiding the nests of smaller birds, it's important to remember that the domestic cat does far more damage to bird populations. The Magpie population has boomed in the last few years, probably because gamekeepers no longer wage war on the species.

IDENTIFICATION

With its striking black-and-white plumage and long tail, it would be hard to mistake the Magpie for any other garden bird. But take a closer look, and you will see that the 'black' is in fact composed of subtle shades of glossy green and purple. Powerful, black bill. Call a far-carrying, harsh, grating rattle, often used to signal alarm.

IN THE GARDEN

STATUS AND HABITAT: Like other members of the crow family, the Magpie has learned to live alongside people, although it still keeps a wary eye open and will rarely allow a close approach. A common visitor to gardens in most parts of Britain, though absent from most of north and west Scotland. In recent years has increased in numbers without spreading in range. A sociable bird, the Magpie forms flocks of between two and a dozen or more birds.

The Magpie is a handsome and intelligent bird, although hated by many householders because of its habit of preying on eggs and chicks of songbirds. In recent years Magpies have become more common, and are often seen in large flocks.

Magpies are adaptable feeders, often visiting bird tables, where they dominate smaller birds. This bird has seized a lump of fat, which will provide much-needed energy.

BREEDING: Breeds from March to September, building an untidy nest from sticks, often prominently on view in the tops of a tree. Lays 5–8 eggs, pale greenish-blue with large brown blotches, and incubates for 17–18 days. Young fledge after 22–28 days. One brood.

FEEDING: Feeds on a wide variety of food, including insects, plants and kitchen scraps. Will also take young chicks from nests.

JACKDAW

Corvus monedula Length 33 cm (13 in)

One of the most attractive and delightful members of the crow family, the Jackdaw is also highly intelligent. Along with the Rook, the Jackdaw is perhaps the bird most characteristic of English village life. There can hardly be a church tower in the country which doesn't harbour a colony of these noisy, sociable birds.

IDENTIFICATION

A small, neat crow, easily told apart from other 'black' crows by its diminutive size and pale grey patch on the back of the head. Plumage otherwise basically black, though slightly lighter on the flanks and chest. Short, thick black bill. In flight appears more compact and shorter-winged than Carrion Crow. Call a characteristic, metallic 'chak' that gives the species its name.

Above: *Mainly a bird of rural and suburban areas, the Jackdaw's attractive appearance and cheeky habits make it one of the most popular members of the crow family.*

Left: *The Jackdaw gets its name from its characteristic call: a harsh "chack chack". Smaller than the Carrion Crow and Rook, it can easily be told apart by its distinctive grey nape.*

IN THE GARDEN

STATUS AND HABITAT: The Jackdaw is a familiar bird of villages, parks and lowland farms throughout the British Isles, apart from the extreme north and west of Scotland. A gregarious bird, it often gathers in noisy flocks, visiting gardens or perching on roofs.
BREEDING: Breeds from April to July, in colonies, often in or near a large building such as a church. Usually nests in a hole or cavity, though sometimes builds a nest from sticks. Lays 4–6 eggs, pale bluish-green with darker blotches, and incubates for 17–18 days. Young fledge after 4–5 weeks. One brood.
FEEDING: Feeds on a wide variety of different foods, including that provided by humans.

ROOK

Corvus frugilegus Length 47 cm (18.5 in)

The typical bird of lowland farmland across most of the country, the Rook is best known for its communal nesting habits. Rookeries are perhaps the easiest of all bird nests to see, especially early in the season when they stand out in silhouette against the bare twigs of trees. Rooks are also celebrated for their 'tumbling' behaviour in autumn, which is supposed to predict the coming of stormy weather.

IDENTIFICATION

A large, all-black crow, distinguished from its close relative the Carrion Crow by its sharp, greyish-white beak, and more peak-shaped crown. In silhouette or in flight, differences in shape also apparent, the Rook having a smaller head, and 'looser-looking' wings. Close views reveal a bright bluish-purple tone to the plumage, especially apparent in bright sunlight. Call a characteristic 'caw'.

The Rook can be told apart from the similar-sized Carrion Crow by its sharp, greyish-white bill and face. It is generally found in rural areas, where it feeds in large flocks on farmland.

Rooks are sociable birds, building untidy nests out of twigs in communal 'rookeries'. They nest early in the year, often before the leaves are back on the trees.

IN THE GARDEN

STATUS AND HABITAT: Less likely to visit gardens than its relatives, the Rook is mainly confined to farmland. However, in rural areas it may frequently be seen in flight overhead.

BREEDING: Breeds from March to July, nesting colonially in large rookeries. Nest built from sticks, though often reuses old nest. Lays 3–6 eggs, pale bluish-green blotched with brown, and incubates for 16–18 days. Young fledge after 29–33 days. One brood in a season.

FEEDING: Feeds mainly on grain and invertebrates such as earthworms.

CARRION/HOODED CROW

Corvus corone Length 47 cm (18.5 in)

At first sight, Carrion and Hooded Crows appear to belong to two quite different species. Yet in fact they are well-marked races of the same species, with the Hooded replacing the more widespread Carrion Crow in north and west Scotland and the whole of Ireland. It is believed that the two races evolved during the last Ice Age, when they became separated, and developed their distinctive plumages.

With its contrasting black and grey plumage, the Hooded Crow looks very different from its southern counterpart, the Carrion Crow. Hooded crows are confined to the extreme north and west of Britain, though they are also found throughout Ireland.

IDENTIFICATION

Carrion Crow is *the* all-black crow, lacking any trace of grey or white in its plumage. Hooded has a black head, throat and upper breast, black wings and tail; the rest of the plumage is pale grey. Both are large, noisy, sociable crows, with powerful, heavy, black bills. Call identical: a harsh 'caw'. Mixed pairs and hybrids often occur in areas where their ranges overlap.

IN THE GARDEN

STATUS AND HABITAT: Carrion Crows are frequent and regular visitors to gardens, especially where food is provided for birds. In larger gardens they may breed. Hooded Crows also visit gardens, though their range is confined to more rural areas than the more widespread race.

BREEDING: Breeds from March to July, building a large, untidy nest from twigs in a tree, though both races also nest on cliffs and even on the ground. Lays 4–6 eggs, pale bluish-green, heavily blotched dark, and incubates for 17–21 days. Young fledge after 4–5 weeks. One brood.

FEEDING: Feeds on almost anything, including seeds, invertebrates, and eggs and young of other birds, though despite its name, rarely takes carrion.

The Carrion Crow breeds in a wide range of sites, building a cup of twigs lined with wool, hair, grass and feathers. The nest is usually easy to see, especially when high in a tree.

140

STARLING

Sturnus vulgaris Length 21 cm (8 in)

A noisy, sociable bird, the Starling is a familiar visitor to gardens, frequently feeding on lawns. Starlings are excellent mimics, imitating not just other birds but also telephones, doorbells and even car alarms! In recent years the Starling has begun to decline in parts of Europe, although the British population appears to be holding its own.

IDENTIFICATION

A mainly dark, medium-sized bird, with a sharp, pointed bill and spotted plumage. Head and underparts blue-black, with a purplish sheen, especially in summer. Sharp, yellow bill. In spring, males appear brighter and less spotted than females, with a blue base to the bill. Juveniles basically dull brown, without spots. Wide variety of calls, including whistles, clicks and wheezy notes. Song very varied, often including mimicry of natural and man-made sounds.

Juvenile Starlings can confuse the novice birdwatcher, as they bear only a slight resemblance to their parents. They are paler than the adults, with a dark bill and a variable amount of spotting.

IN THE GARDEN

STATUS AND HABITAT: A regular and common garden visitor throughout the British Isles, in both rural and urban settings. Starlings are adaptable birds, and will readily take food from all kinds of sources. In winter, large influxes of birds from the European continent surge into southern and eastern Britain.

BREEDING: Breeds from April to September, nesting in any suitable holes or crevices. Lays 4–7 pale blue eggs, and incubates for 12–15 days. Young fledge after 20–22 days. One, sometimes two broods in a season. Males can be polygynous, and have been known to pair with up to five different females.

FEEDING: Feeds mainly on invertebrates, taken from soil in grassy areas. Will also take a wide variety of food provided by humans.

With its glossy black plumage, bright yellow bill and sociable habits, the Starling is a familiar garden visitor. They normally feed in large, noisy flocks, squabbling with each other and fighting off smaller species.

HOUSE SPARROW

Passer domesticus Length 15 cm (6 in)

Of all Britain's birds, the House Sparrow is surely the species most closely associated with humankind. A sociable bird, it is easily overlooked yet endlessly fascinating. House Sparrows have recently begun to decline in many rural areas, so gardens may prove to be an important stronghold in the future.

IDENTIFICATION

The archetypal small brown bird, though on a closer view handsome and colourful. Male has grey crown and nape, edged with chocolate-brown on sides of head, black bib and dirty white cheeks. Upperparts a rich mixture of browns, buffs and greys, with white wingbar. Underparts dingy grey. Female much duller, with tawny upperparts edged with black, buffish-grey underparts, and broad creamy-buff stripe above and behind the eye. Best-known call a metallic 'cheep', often uttered by several birds at once.

IN THE GARDEN

STATUS AND HABITAT: One of the commonest and most widespread garden visitors, especially in urban areas and near arable farms. Sparrow flocks often

The male House Sparrow is a distinctive and handsome bird, with a grey crown and black bib contrasting with whitish cheeks. The larger the male's bib, the more successful he is at attracting females.

draw attention by their noisy, squabbling behaviour, especially when competing for food. Most abundant in the south and east of the British Isles.

BREEDING: Breeds from April to August, nesting mainly in holes, especially beneath roof tiles, where noisy colonies may cause a disturbance. Lays 3–6 eggs, pale with brown and grey speckles, and incubates for 11–14 days. Young fledge after 14–19 days. Often raises three or even four broods.

FEEDING: Feeds mainly on insects in summer, and grain in winter, although will also take a wide variety of food provided by humans. Often displaces Blue and Great Tits from peanut-feeders.

In contrast to the male, the female House Sparrow is rather a dull-looking bird, although at close range the subtle shades of brown and grey can be seen.

TREE SPARROW

Passer montanus Length 14 cm (5.5 in)

Superficially resembles its close cousin the House Sparrow, but their lifestyles and fortunes could hardly be more different. The Tree Sparrow is primarily a bird of lowland farmland, and in recent years has suffered a catastrophic fall in numbers. If the decline continues, this charming and attractive species could even face extinction as a British breeding bird.

IDENTIFICATION

Looks like a brighter, cleaner, more attractive version of House Sparrow. Best distinguished by chocolate-brown cap (grey-and-brown in the House Sparrow), broad white collar, and a dark black spot on the cheek. Also has whiter cheeks, smaller black bib and overall brighter, more rufous upperparts than House Sparrow. Underparts buffish. Sexes alike. Call a quiet 'tek-tek'.

IN THE GARDEN

STATUS AND HABITAT: Mainly associated with arable farmland, the Tree Sparrow has never been a common visitor to gardens, although it will readily feed on nuts from artificial feeders when available. Most likely to be seen in parts of rural southern and eastern Britain, and largely absent from south-west England, west Wales, and most of Ireland and Scotland. Mainly sedentary.

BREEDING: Breeds from April to August, nesting mainly in hedgerows. Lays 4–6 eggs, buff with dark spots, and incubates for 11–14 days. Young fledge after 12–14 days. Often two or even three broods. Tree Sparrows can be encouraged to use nestboxes.

FEEDING: Feeds on invertebrates during breeding season and on seeds during the rest of the year. Will also feed on peanuts.

Above: *This close-up view shows the chocolate-brown cap, white collar and black spot behind the eye that distinguish the Tree Sparrow from the House Sparrow. Like its commoner relative, the Tree Sparrow often feeds in gardens, with a preference for seed and peanut feeders.*

Right: *The Tree Sparrow has recently suffered a major decline in numbers and range, mainly as a result of modern farming practices. Unlike the House Sparrow, the male and female are alike.*

CHAFFINCH

Fringilla coelebs Length 15.5 cm (6 in)

One of Britain's most numerous breeding birds, the Chaffinch is comparatively unknown to many people, as it is mainly found in wooded areas and farmland. In parts of rural Britain, especially Scotland, the Chaffinch is the commonest small bird, often forming huge flocks during the winter months, when it feeds on stubble fields.

With his bright orange-pink underparts and white wingbars, the male Chaffinch is one of our most attractive garden birds. It is also one of the commonest, found throughout the British Isles, being especially common in rural areas.

IDENTIFICATION

With his striking pink underparts, bluish-grey head, and white wing-patches, the male Chaffinch is one of our most handsome and distinctive small birds. Female a duller version of male, with brown back, dark wings with white patches, and buff underparts. Female can sometimes be confused with female House Sparrow, but distinguished by wing-pattern, overall neater appearance and sharp, conical bill. In flight, both sexes reveal a moss-green rump. Best-known call a loud 'pink', from which the name 'finch' derives. Song an accelerating series of notes with a flourish at the end – once described as 'like a fast bowler running up to deliver'.

IN THE GARDEN

STATUS AND HABITAT: A familiar garden visitor, especially in rural and suburban areas, throughout Britain. Often feeds on open lawns. In winter Chaffinches move from woodland breeding areas onto farmland, frequently in the company of sparrows and buntings, as well as other finches.

BREEDING: Breeds from April to July, nesting mainly in the fork of a suitable bush or tree. Lays 3–5 eggs, pale blue with darker spots, and incubates for 11–13 days. Young fledge after 12–15 days. One, occasionally two, broods in a season.

FEEDING: Feeds mainly on a diet of insects in spring and summer, and on a variety of seeds and berries during the rest of the year.

The female Chaffinch superficially resembles a female House Sparrow, but can be distinguished by her white wingbars and sharp, cone-shaped bill. Like the male, in flight she reveals a bright green rump.

BRAMBLING

Fringilla montifringilla Length 15.5 cm (6 in)

The northern equivalent of the Chaffinch, the Brambling is almost exclusively a winter visitor to the British Isles from its breeding-grounds in Scandinavia and northern Russia. Some years there are relatively few, while others bring huge invasions of birds in search of their favourite food, beech mast. Often seen in mixed flocks with other finches, sparrows and buntings.

IN THE GARDEN

STATUS AND HABITAT: Winter visitor, arriving in September–October and leaving in April. Found throughout rural Britain, apart from north-west Scotland and parts of west Wales. Scarce in Ireland. May visit gardens in the company of other finches, especially during hard weather, when it prefers to feed on seeds scattered on the ground. Commonest near large beech woods or farmland with hedgerows.
FEEDING: Feeds on seeds, especially beech mast.

IDENTIFICATION

Superficially similar to Chaffinch, the Brambling is easily told apart by its darker back, rusty-orange on the breast, yellowish bill, and in flight, a bright white rump. Male in winter has dark head and upper back, dark wings with white wingbars, rusty-orange breast and white belly. They also have a yellowish bill with dark tip. Female looks like duller version of male, with brown and grey head-pattern, and much more subdued orange on breast and wings. In flight dark wings and back contrast with white rump. Call, often uttered in flight, is a soft 'yup'.

Above: *A winter visitor to Britain, often in large numbers from its northern breeding-grounds, the Brambling is one of our most welcome garden visitors. The male is a brightly-coloured bird, with a black-and-orange plumage and bright white rump, revealed in flight.*

Left: *The female Brambling is slightly duller than the male, with a less contrasting head pattern. Bramblings feed mainly on beech mast, so they are most likely to be encountered in wooded, rural gardens.*

SERIN

Serinus serinus Length 11 cm (4 in)

This tiny finch is a familiar sight and sound throughout rural areas of Europe, where it frequently lives in villages, singing its jangling song from a tree, post or telegraph wire. Despite spreading rapidly north during the last few decades it remains a very rare and sporadic breeding bird in Britain, where it has nested in southern coastal counties from Devon to Sussex.

IDENTIFICATION

A small, plump, compact finch, with a large head and tiny, stubby bill. Male has bright yellow head, face and throat, with darker green crown and cheeks. Upperparts greyish-green, with dark streaks. Underparts yellow on breast, shading to white on belly, with dark streaks on flanks. Female much duller, with streaked greenish-grey plumage and pale underparts. Song a rapid, scratchy jangle, delivered either from a perch or in song-flight.

IN THE GARDEN

STATUS AND HABITAT: A characteristic bird of parks and gardens, especially in rural areas, throughout continental Europe. Has bred in southern England, and as global warming takes hold is a likely contender for permanent colonisation as a British

Europe's smallest finch, the Serin makes up in character what it lacks in size. In spring, males sing their characteristic jangling song from prominent posts or wires.

breeding bird. Partial migrant, wintering mainly around the Mediterranean, but some southern populations resident.

BREEDING: Breeds from April to August, building well-concealed nest in deep vegetation such as ornamental conifers. Lays 3–5 eggs, pale blue with dark spots, and incubates for 13 days. Young fledge after 13–17 days. Two broods.

FEEDING: Feeds mainly on weed seeds; but also takes insects during the breeding season.

The Serin has extended its range north and westwards in recent years, although it has yet to cross the Channel to breed in any numbers. On the continent, however, it is one of the most characteristic sights and sounds of village life.

GREENFINCH

Carduelis chloris Length 15 cm (6 in)

The harsh, wheezy call of the male Greenfinch often alerts you to his presence, perched high in the tops of a tall tree or bush. Greenfinches have adapted well to gardens, and often prefer to nest and roost in introduced plants such as cypresses, whose dense foliage provides excellent cover. They also readily take advantage of hanging peanut feeders.

IDENTIFICATION

The male Greenfinch certainly lives up to his name, sporting a bright yellowish-green plumage, relieved only by grey and yellow on the wings and a dark tail. Females are much duller, sometimes appearing almost grey, though always showing some trace of green and yellow in the plumage. Juveniles also dull, with dark streaks on underparts. Stout, powerful bill, typical of a seed–eater.

The female Greenfinch is duller than the male, but still shows enough green and yellow in the plumage to be easily identified. Greenfinches often breed in ornamental conifers, which provide the dense foliage to conceal their nest.

IN THE GARDEN

STATUS AND HABITAT: A common and familiar garden bird throughout the British Isles, often breeding in thick foliage, especially evergreens. In winter, forms flocks. These often visit bird-tables, where they feed mainly on peanuts and seeds, often aggressively jostling for position.

BREEDING: Breeds from April to August, often nesting in loose colonies. Lays 3–6 eggs, pale with a few dark spots, and incubates for 12–14 days. Young fledge after 13–17 days. Two, occasionally three, broods.

FEEDING: Feeds mainly on seeds, though will eat insects in summer, and nuts and fruit in winter. Feeds readily from artificial feeders.

The male Greenfinch often sings his harsh, wheezy song from a prominent position on a bush or tree. Greenfinches show a marked preference for peanut feeders, often appearing in small flocks.

GOLDFINCH

Carduelis carduelis Length 14 cm (5.5 in)

A flock of Goldfinches, with their tinkling calls and bright, colourful plumage, is quite appropriately known as a 'charm'. This delightful little finch is most likely to visit your garden if you let an area grow wild, and plant thistles and teasels. These produce the Goldfinch's favourite food, tiny seeds, which it extracts with its sharp, pointed bill.

IDENTIFICATION

Once seen well, unmistakable: a delightful combination of pale brown, black, gold and red, producing a flurry of colour and movement, especially in flight. Sexes alike: buffish-brown back; underparts brown, mixed with white on breast and belly; wings black with dazzling gold stripe; and bright crimson-red patch on face. Juvenile lacks red on face. Often heard before seen: flocks give incessant, musical twittering, especially in flight.

A close-up view of the adult Goldfinch reveals the extraordinary beauty of its plumage: the crimson face, dark wings and dazzling gold flash which gives the species its name.

Goldfinches have a specially-adapted, sharp, conical bill, enabling them to probe deep into plants such as the teasel to remove the seeds. Letting part of your garden grow wild will provide the right habitat to attract these delightful birds.

IN THE GARDEN

STATUS AND HABITAT: A widespread visitor to gardens, especially outside the breeding-season, when flocks travel widely in search of food. British-breeding Goldfinches head south to France and Spain in winter, with large numbers of continental birds arriving to take their place.

BREEDING: Breeds from April to August, building a small cup of grass, often on the outermost twigs of a tree. Lays 4–6 eggs (pale, with a few spots and streaks) and incubates for 12–14 days. Young fledge after 12–15 days. Two, occasionally three, broods in a season.

FEEDING: Outside the breeding season, feeds almost exclusively on weed seeds. During the breeding season will also take insects. In recent years has begun to come to garden feeders in greater numbers.

SISKIN

Carduelis spinus Length 12 cm (4.5 in)

In recent years, this small black-and-green finch has become a familiar late winter visitor to gardens throughout the country, showing a marked preference for peanuts in red-coloured bags or feeders, which are thought to resemble its natural food of alder cones. Its extraordinary rise has been aided by the spread of coniferous forests, in which Siskins usually breed.

IDENTIFICATION

A small, compact, fork-tailed finch, with a predominantly streaked plumage of green, black and yellow, and a sharp, pointed bill. Male brighter than female, with black cap, crown and throat, yellow neck and breast, pale belly with dark streaks on flanks, and green back streaked lightly with black. Wings black with yellow bars, tail black with yellow patches on sides, and deep fork at tip. Female looks like dull version of male, lacking black on head and most yellow tones. Juvenile like pale female, with more streaks. Various twittering calls, often uttered by several individuals in flock.

IN THE GARDEN

STATUS AND HABITAT: Mainly a winter visitor to gardens, especially frequent in February and March when natural food becomes scarce. Often travels in flocks, which appear suddenly, feed for a few minutes, then are gone.

BREEDING: Breeds mainly in coniferous forests away from gardens.

FEEDING: Feeds on seeds and insects, mainly from conifers such as spruce and alders. However, has recently developed a taste for peanuts, especially those in red-coloured feeders.

Above: *The female Siskin is a duller bird than the male, lacking the distinctive black on the head. Siskins have recently undergone a population explosion, and often visit gardens in flocks, especially during the winter and spring.*

Right: *In the breeding season, the adult male Siskin is one of our most attractive finches, with his black crown and forehead, and green and yellow plumage. Siskins feed mainly on alder cones, though will also readily take peanuts, especially from red feeders.*

LINNET

Carduelis cannabina Length 14 cm (5.5 in)

Once a popular Victorian cage bird celebrated in music-hall tradition, the Linnet is best-known for its melodious and delicate song, perhaps the closest native equivalent to that of the Canary. In autumn and winter it forms large flocks, often feeding on stubble-fields with other finches and buntings. Like many other farmland birds, it is currently undergoing a rapid and sudden population decline.

With his bright breeding plumage and delightful song, it comes as no surprise that the male Linnet was a popular cagebird in Victorian times. Today, along with other farmland birds, the Linnet faces a new threat: a population decline caused by modern farming methods.

IDENTIFICATION

A small, neat finch with a small, conical bill. In the breeding season, the male is unmistakable, sporting bright crimson patches on the forehead and sides of the breast. However, in winter, both sexes are a rather dull-looking brownish colour. Males have a reddish-brown back, dark wings, a grey-brown head and lightly streaked brown underparts. Females are greyer, with less rufous in the plumage. Juveniles pale buff with dark streaks. Often seen in flight, identified by its light, melodious twittering call, and pale flashes on the wings.

IN THE GARDEN

STATUS AND HABITAT: Mainly associated with lowland farmland, so not a very common visitor to gardens. In recent years numbers have begun to decline as a result of modern farming methods. In winter, mainly confined to southern and eastern Britain, and to areas near the coasts.

BREEDING: Breeds from April to August, often in loose colonies. Lays 4–6 eggs, pale with reddish spots, and incubates for 10–14 days. Young fledge after 11–13 days. Two, sometimes three, broods.

FEEDING: Feeds on insects in spring and summer, and seeds during the rest of the year.

Outside the breeding season, Linnets appear rather dull, and are best identified by their rapid, twittering call. This first-winter bird shows the typical streaky brown plumage and small, pointed bill.

REDPOLL

Carduelis flammea Length 12–13 cm (4.5–5 in)

The bright patch of colour on the male bird's forehead gives this attractive little finch its name. Like the Siskin, it often gathers in winter flocks to feed, though it is a far less frequent visitor to gardens. Some winters see invasions of large numbers of the northern race, known as 'Mealy' Redpoll, from Scandinavia.

IDENTIFICATION

A small, rather dumpy finch, superficially resembling the Linnet, though generally darker and with a streakier plumage. Male has crimson patch on forehead. Female shows much less red on forehead. Both sexes have tiny, pointed bill; small, neat, black bib; and two buff wingbars. Upperparts brown, streaked with buff; underparts greyish-white, with dark streaks along flanks. Rump pale; tail dark. Birds from north European race, known as 'Mealy' Redpoll, are larger and paler than British birds, with extensive amounts of white in the plumage. Often feeds by hanging acrobatically from twigs as it extracts the seeds from cones and catkins. Soft, two-syllable call.

Above: *Like most finches, the female Redpoll is duller than the male, although the crimson forehead can still be seen. Redpolls often form flocks, sometimes accompanying their close relative, the Siskin.*

Below: *This Redpoll, drinking from a convenient pool, shows the crimson forehead that gives the species its name. During the breeding season, males also show a pinkish tinge on the breast.*

IN THE GARDEN

STATUS AND HABITAT: Although they breed widely in northern and eastern parts of Britain, Redpolls are most likely to be seen in gardens during the winter months. They are particularly partial to birch and alder seeds. They may accompany flocks of Siskins.

BREEDING: Breeds mainly in woodlands of birch, alder and conifer, generally away from garden areas.

FEEDING: Feeds on insects in summer, and mainly on seeds during the winter.

BULLFINCH

Pyrrhula pyrrhula Length 16 cm (6.5 in)

With its bright, cherry-red plumage, conspicuous white rump and huge bill, the male Bullfinch is one of our most striking and attractive small birds. Feeding mainly on the buds of fruit-trees, it is a lot less popular with market-gardeners than with birdwatchers. Like other farmland species, it is currently undergoing a rapid decline in population.

IDENTIFICATION

Male unmistakable: stout shape, bright cherry-pink underparts, black face and head, bluish-grey back, black tail and wings with white wingbar. Female looks like browner version of male, with buffish-brown back and underparts. Juvenile lacks black on head. Characteristic call: a soft, low whistle.

IN THE GARDEN

STATUS AND HABITAT: A regular visitor in small numbers to gardens, especially in rural areas near woodland or fruit-growing areas. Most likely to be seen in the south and east of the country. Mainly resident, although some years see an invasion of Scandinavian birds, whose plumage is even brighter than the British race.

The male Bullfinch is quite simply unmistakable: no other bird has his combination of cherry-pink underparts, black face and head, and huge bill. Like many species associated with farmland, the Bullfinch has recently undergone a rapid and serious decline.

BREEDING: Breeds from May to August, nesting in thick scrub. Lays 3–6 eggs, pale blue with a few black spots, and incubates for 12–14 days. Young fledge after 15–17 days. Two, sometimes three, broods in a season.

FEEDING: Feeds mainly on seeds, though in spring will also take insects and buds of fruit-trees.

The female Bullfinch lacks the male's bright pink breast, but otherwise shows the same plumage features. In flight, Bullfinches can be distinguished by their bright white rump and characteristic piping call.

HAWFINCH

Coccothraustes coccothraustes Length 18 cm (7 in)

Despite its large size, massive bill and striking plumage, this beautiful and striking finch is one of the shyest and most elusive of all our woodland birds. It is an occasional winter visitor to gardens, especially those near woodlands. Hawfinches have a preference for particular kinds of tree: especially hornbeam and cherry, whose seeds it can crack open with its extraordinary bill.

IDENTIFICATION

A massive, bulky finch, with a vast bill built to crack hard seeds. Head, neck and underparts a rich, chestnut-brown, duller and greyer in female. Face-pattern has black bib and thick black stripe in front of the eye, less prominent in female. Back darker brown, with broad white wingbar and purplish-blue wings. In flight, the striking black-and-white wing pattern is usually obvious. Emits a loud, explosive 'zik, zik', often in flight, so may be heard before it is seen.

IN THE GARDEN

STATUS AND HABITAT: Hawfinches have a patchy distribution in Britain, being found in large areas of mixed woodland, especially beech and hornbeam, mainly in the southern and eastern regions of England. They are most likely to visit gardens in rural areas, and during hard weather in winter, when they may also feed on berries.

BREEDING: Breeds in large, undisturbed areas of mixed woodland, away from gardens.

FEEDING: Feeds on seeds, berries and fruit, including cherry-stones, hornbeam and beech nuts.

Above: *A shy bird, the Hawfinch is rarely seen away from its woodland haunts, although it may occasionally pay a visit to rural gardens. This female was photographed at a pond in Kent.*

Left: *The Hawfinch – Britain's largest finch – uses its massive bill for crushing seeds to feed on their kernels. The male is slightly brighter than the female, with a more prominent black bib and a more strongly marked wing-pattern.*

YELLOWHAMMER

Emberiza citrinella Length 16.5 cm (6.5 in)

With its characteristic song, 'A-little-bit-of-bread-and-no-cheese', and striking yellow and brown plumage, the Yellowhammer is one of the best-known birds of rural Britain. As with other farmland species, however, it is currently undergoing a major population decline. Yellowhammers often sing throughout the summer, continuing after many other birds have fallen silent.

IDENTIFICATION

The adult male Yellowhammer is, given good views, unmistakable. A long, slim bunting, with a sulphur-yellow head streaked with light brown. Upperparts and rump chestnut-brown, streaked darker on the back. Breast chestnut, shading to pale on belly. Female is much duller, browner and streakier, especially on head and breast. Occasionally females and juveniles show very little yellow in the plumage, and may be confused with other species of bunting or sparrow.

The female Yellowhammer resembles a duller version of the male, and may show very little yellow in her plumage. Yellowhammers are mainly a bird of arable farmland, though may sometimes visit gardens, especially during harsh winter weather.

IN THE GARDEN

STATUS AND HABITAT: During the breeding season and winter months, Yellowhammers are generally dependent on farmland for food, so are rarely seen in gardens except for those in rural farming areas. During hard winter weather, however, they may join mixed flocks of finches and buntings in search of food from bird-tables, often feeding on spilt seed on the ground. Commoner in the south and east of the country, and becoming very rare in Ireland.

BREEDING: Breeds mainly on farmland, away from gardens.

FEEDING: Feeds on insects during the breeding season; seeds and berries during the rest of the year.

A member of the bunting family, the Yellowhammer is best-known for its song. The male in breeding plumage is a striking bird, with his bright yellow head contrasting with darker body and chestnut rump.

Reed Bunting

Emberiza schoeniclus Length 15.5 cm (6 in)

Although mainly associated with wetland areas during the breeding season, in the autumn and winter months Reed Buntings roam far and wide, often visiting gardens with other seed-eating birds, and feeding readily from bird tables and on the ground. Undergoing a recent rapid population decline, probably due to lack of available food in winter.

During the winter, Reed Buntings leave their reedbed haunts and feed in flocks on farmland. In hard weather they will also visit gardens, occasionally taking food from feeders and bird tables.

IDENTIFICATION

Breeding-plumage male has unique and striking head-pattern: all black apart from white 'moustache' and collar. Non-breeding males and females far less distinctive, although traces of the head-pattern remain and can usually be seen. White moustache, black on sides of chin and white throat usually obvious. Otherwise this bird looks like a bright sparrow, with upperparts a mixture of chestnut, buff and black streaking; the underparts greyish and lightly streaked with black. Tail dark with white outer feathers, and often quite visible in flight. The call is a thin 'tsee-ooo'.

IN THE GARDEN

STATUS AND HABITAT: In recent years there has been a major increase in garden sightings of Reed Buntings, especially in autumn and winter. At night these birds roost in reedbeds, so they are most likely to be seen in gardens located near water.
BREEDING: Breeds in reedbeds, away from gardens.
FEEDING: Feeds mainly on a wide variety of seeds, especially grass seeds.

The male Reed Bunting is easily identified by his striking black head and throat, contrasting with a bright white collar and moustache. In flight, Reed Buntings also show white outer tail feathers.

FURTHER READING

BOOKS ON GARDEN BIRDS

Burton, Robert, *The RSPB Birdfeeder Handbook* (1991, Dorling Kindersley)

Couzens, Dominic, and Langman, Mike, *The Mitchell Beazley Pocket Guide to Garden Birds* (1996, Mitchell Beazley)

du Feu, Chris, *Nestboxes* (1993, BTO)

Golley, Mark, Moss, Stephen, and Daly, David, *The Complete Garden Bird Book* (1996, New Holland)

Oddie, Bill and Holden, Peter, *Bird in the Nest* (1995, Robson Books)

Snow, Barbara and David, *Birds and Berries* (1988, Poyser)

Soper, Tony, *The Bird Table Book* (1992, David & Charles)

BOOKS ON GARDENING

Baines, Chris, *How to Make a Wildlife Garden* (1996, Elm Tree Books)

Brookes, John, *John Brookes' Garden Design Book* (1991, Dorling Kindersley)

Caplan, Basil, Ed., *The Complete Manual of Organic Gardening* (1995, Headline)

Fearnley-Whittingstall, Jane, *Gardening Made Easy* (1997, Phoenix Illustrated)

Hamilton, Geoff, *The Organic Gardening Book* (1997, Dorling Kindersley)

Newbury, Tim, *The Ultimate Garden Designer* (1995, Ward Lock)

Rees, Yvonne, *Practical Garden Design* (1993, Crowood Press)

Search, Gay, *Gardening from Scratch* (1996, BBC Books)

Squire, David, *The Practical Gardener* (1996, Salamander)

BOOKS ON BIRDS AND BIRDWATCHING

The Complete Book of British Birds (1998, AA/RSPB)

Brooke, Michael, and Tim Birkhead, Ed. *The Cambridge Encyclopedia of Ornithology* (1991, Cambridge University Press)

Jonsson, Lars, *Birds of Europe* (1996, Christopher Helm)

Moss, Stephen, *Birds and Weather* (1995, Hamlyn)

Oddie, Bill, *Bill Oddie's Birds of Britain and Ireland* (1998, New Holland)

Oddie, Bill, and Moss, Stephen, *Birding with Bill Oddie*, (1997, BBC Books)

Sample, Geoff, *Collins Field Guide to Bird Songs and Calls* (1996, HarperCollins)

MAGAZINES

BBC Wildlife
Available monthly from most newsagents, or by subscription from:
BBC Wildlife Subscriptions, PO Box 425, Woking, Surrey GU21 1GP

Birdwatch
Available monthly from larger newsagents, or by subscription from:
Birdwatch (Subs Dept.), Fulham House, Goldsworth Road, Woking, Surrey, GU21 1LY.
Tel: 01483 733886

Bird Watching
Available monthly from larger newsagents, or by subscription from:
Bird Watching subscriptions, Tower Publishing Services Ltd, Tower House, Sovereign Park, Market Harborough, Leics LE16 9EF

British Birds
Available monthly by subscription from:
British Birds (Subscriptions), Fountains, Park Lane, Blunham, Bedford MJK44 3NJ